Etched in Sunlight

25⅜

Rue St. Hilaire, Senlis

ETCHED IN SUNLIGHT

Fifty Years in the
Graphic Arts

by

SAMUEL CHAMBERLAIN, N.A.

BOSTON PUBLIC LIBRARY

MCMLXVIII

The Town Gate, Marvejols,
from *Bouquet de France*

Library of Congress Catalog Card Number: 68-29421

Title page vignette: The Shadowy Street, Senlis (drypoint, 1930)

Printed in the United States of America by The Meriden Gravure Company
Meriden, Connecticut

Château de la Morinière

Contents

Market Day in the Place Nationale, Montauban

Isola Tiberina, Rome

Introduction

SAMUEL CHAMBERLAIN's studies at MIT pointed to a career in architecture. Pursuing that course, he doubtless would have had leisure for some of his later interests in the collecting of books, pictures and furniture, in travel and in the exploration of food and wine. But his interests brimmed over, and his impulses were irrepressibly adventurous. His newly discovered gifts as an artist led him on. Today the wealth of his drawings, drypoints, etchings, lithographs and photographs, and the long bookshelves which attempt to contain all the books he has made over the years, speak for a life in which great diversity of experience has been seized and held and turned to good account. Benjamin Franklin, also a man of many accomplishments and many experiences, a man of the world, good friend and congenial companion, would approve. As an architect of American opinion, he might admire Chamberlain's position as an architect of taste. It is an unintended role, as far as I can see, and an immensely constructive one. In book after book Chamberlain has opened our eyes to our architectural heritage. The awareness that will help to preserve much of it has come in part from him. So has the U. S. A.'s growing awareness of food and drink as elements of civilization which can reflect high standards, a proud history and lively interests in place of dull routine.

The Town Gate, Ammerschwihr

As an artist, Chamberlain's fascination has been with light and line. He likes to see the world in full, three-dimensional contrast of brightness and shadow. His penciled linear detail is sure and accurate, but it does not attempt to be exhaustive.

vii

Huddington Court, Worcestershire,
from *British Bouquet*

Ascoli Piceno, from *Italian Bouquet*

Light and contrast are used to suggest mass and relief. Choosing no little area of subject matter, he has gone far afield in pursuit of the architectural landmarks, mighty and humble, of Europe and the United States.

As a writer, he has evolved a style true to his own person: witty, keenly observant, sympathetic, lingering over the good things of life and getting past the bad ones as speedily as possible. His three monumental guides to travel in France, Italy and Britain are in a class by themselves, mingling anecdote with a sense of geography, landscape and architecture, magnificently illustrated, and with detailed information on restaurants, hotels, food and wine. In an age of picture books, he is the author of scores, and all of them have clear, sharp, unforgettable images that crystallize atmosphere and character and bring the viewer back to look again. A friend tells me that he carried one of Chamberlain's earlier picture books—*Historic Boston in Four Seasons,* published in 1938—all the way to Okinawa in the course of World War II. I can see why.

To the picture books and cookbooks and the three hefty guide books, add a venture in prose, one of the most entertaining books I know, and full of good recipes in the bargain. *Clementine in the Kitchen* seems to be perennially (and deservedly) reprinted. Chamberlain's books have made us better friends of our own country and have helped renew the old bonds of close friendship between the United States and Britain, France and Italy.

Reminiscences by a man who has done so much, and seen so much—and who, moreover, is a professional writer as well as artist—would promise a book of the most interesting sort. But how to get it? Especially from an author who loves work, refuses to retire, and averages a new book a year.

By pure good luck, the Boston Public Library proposed the present book just as Mr. Chamberlain was catching his breath after completing the new edition of *Bouquet de France* in the summer of 1966. With minor chores on the calendar for the coming months, he was making plans for a vacation and saw an opportunity, after that, to put on paper an account of fifty years in the graphic arts. Travel, food, wine, book collecting and other interests could not be left out of the story, and neither party to the agreement wanted them left out. We at the Boston Public Library are deeply grateful for the narrative which has resulted.

The idea for the book developed naturally from the Library's collection of Chamberlain's graphic work. During 1966 we were in the process of broadening the collection to give a better reflection of the range of the artist's talents. We were buying

The Tombs of the Caliphs, Egypt

the first of his photographs to come into this collection, many of them big mat-finish enlargements of American and European subjects. But even with an excellent collection of his etchings, drypoints and lithographs, and a good beginning collection of his photographs and drawings, the evidence of his knowledge of the art of the book remained untouched.

However accurate a reproduction of a drawing, print or photograph may be, it will never be the same as the original—a stubborn truth Chamberlain has accepted in his planning of books. He has also known, however, that as a picture a reproduction can be good in itself. His picture books sparkle with contrasts. Many of them have a richness of tone in some ways comparable to the depth of color possible in an etching sympathetically wiped in a warm ink and printed on an appropriate paper. The black-and-white reproductions in his books capture light. He knows the results he wants, and to get them he has sought out the best technical processes and the best craftsmen available. All of this is part of the story we asked him to tell. It can be told only in a volume in which pictures and text are full partners.

The Pyramids

A Roman Remnant in Africa

The Village Church, Roberval

During the time in which he was choosing pictures for these pages, we suggested several areas of his work which we believe deserve special emphasis. To know the fundamentals of his art, you must see his pencil drawings. Two series which may be little-known, in the originals, are the studies of French brick buildings, drawn in the twenties and thirties, and the drawings of North African and Egyptian architecture and landscape made during World War II. The French drawings are uncanny in their successful attempt to combine an empirical assignment—suggesting with a pencil the weight and size of bricks in the fabric of buildings often both large and elaborate —with the artist's suggestive approach to light, atmosphere, distance, and necessarily, too, of detail. Every brick in every façade couldn't have been shown even if showing them had been desirable. The drawings don't try—but to my amateur's eye, they triumph in both their objects, empirical and artistic. The North African and Egyptian drawings bring the character of sunbaked landscape and a long, rich architectural tradition very close.

A liberal sampling from each of these series of drawings is included in this book, and great pains have been taken to bring the reproductions as close to the originals as possible. This is easiest when there is a full page to work with. We have tried to be generous in the number of full-page illustrations; some of them make possible the reproduction of drawings actual size.

A third group of drawings which to me tells something about Chamberlain's mingling of artistic gifts with a love of architecture are the studies of German gun emplacements in Italian towns, drawn during World War II as aids to American photo intelligence. The architectural details—elevations, ground plans, etc.—are meticulous, but on top of all is a lovingly drawn bit of Italian townscape and countryscape, showing the fortifications as they fitted into their setting. I feel sure that the Air Force had only one artist at its service who could produce this particular combination of details in this way. Some of these drawings are reproduced, too, in the course of Mr. Chamberlain's account.

To the publishers, the author's ability to be his own typographer is, for this autobiographical volume, the frosting on the cake. Possessing the necessary skills and experience, he chose the page size, selected the type face, devised the format, defined the sizes of the reproductions, and sought the qualities in reproduction which he felt were truest to his original pictures. His detailed layout revealed a book-architect of long standing. Aiding and abetting the enterprise have been Harold Hugo,

John Peckham and William Glick of The Meriden Gravure Company, Meriden, Connecticut. They gave generously of their time; their unfailing helpfulness and the hospitality and kindness of Mr. and Mrs. Parker Allen make us feel that The Meriden Gravure Company is a unique institution indeed. Warren Skillings of The Anthoensen Press, Portland, Maine, has seen to the typesetting, and we are indebted to him for excellent, thoughtful service. Lucia Blackwelder of the Boston Public Library Print Department made the smooth typed copy of the text from which type was set, and Edith Payne of the Print Department prepared a comprehensive first draft of the index.

Mrs. Chamberlain has been foremost among a group of allies who kindly read copy and proof. She, Boston Public Library Director Philip McNiff, Mrs. McNiff, Mrs. Sherburne Prescott and David McCord all read and commented on the initial typescript. To Marie O'Donnell we extend thanks for helping in the reading of galley proofs.

Finally, the Library is grateful to a group of friends who helped with funds which made up part of the capital needed to underwrite this venture in intimate history, interweaving words and pictures.

Farm Gate in the Oise

Of all the terms that might be used to describe Samuel Chamberlain, *humanist* is one that fits. The human dimensions of his narrative have made it a great pleasure to help see this book into print.

SINCLAIR H. HITCHINGS,
Keeper of Prints, Boston Public Library

Château de Montigny

Narthex and Nave of the Church of the Madeleine, Vézelay

Normandy Cottage, Notre-Dame de Bliquetuit

MANY workers in the graphic arts are quiet, unspectacular people. They travel, of course, but appear to be happiest when working undisturbed in their studios, free to print their copperplates or wood blocks or lithographic stones without interruption. Most of them are retiring and industrious fellows who enjoy the simple things in life—a family and friends, good books and music, good food and wine. Self-effacing is perhaps not the expression to describe them, but neither are they flamboyant or extrovert. In short, this is not at all the sort of person that lends well to biographical treatment.

It came as a considerable surprise, therefore, to be considered by the eminent print authorities of the Boston Public Library as a fitting subject for a book. At first, this printmaker was beset by doubt. What did my mild, unglamorous career have to offer? Still, more than half a century *had* elapsed since my debut as a pencil sketcher and watercolorist. Many artistic ups and downs are certain to unfold in such a lengthy span.

Other strands run through the twisted twine of those years, family and friends first of all. Prominent also is a lifelong interest in book collecting and gastronomy, but these are rather foreign to the central

Gateway in Montepillois, Oise

I

The Rogers Building, Boston

The Customs Tower, Boston

theme of the graphic arts. Inextricably woven into the same skein, however, is a joyous enthusiasm for architecture. What follows is essentially the account of an architectural draftsman gone slightly astray. Any number of sculptors, decorators, typographers, book designers, engineers and construction supervisors have received their first impetus from an architectural education. They veer from the path of architectural rectitude and branch out into a related field. Printmakers are no exception. They have been taught to draw, to perceive beauty, to detect the spurious, and to glory in the radiance of nature. A fine basic training is already theirs.

Faneuil Hall, Boston

Encouraged to poke into old portfolios, clipping files and solander boxes, I found enough semiforgotten manuscripts, watercolors, pencil sketches, lithographs and etchings to conjure up all sorts of reminiscences. The proposal to write about my half century in the graphic arts suddenly ceased to be preposterous. Now, with some hesitation, I am bold enough to accept the invitation to relate that story briefly, aided by illustrations.

As the curtain rises on the career of this particular graphic artist, you behold a shy and somewhat bewildered young man from the Pacific coast on a September day in 1915. He was just under twenty at the time, a newly arrived sophomore in the School of Architecture at

3

The Great Court,
MIT in Cambridge

the Massachusetts Institute of Technology in Boston, and he was in a large studio illuminated by frosted overhead windows, attending his first life class. Blushing furiously in the presence of a languid and most undraped Boston model named Bernice, the young man sensed that his ear lobes were hot, and that he had no ability to appear unconcerned, or to set down his impressions of the nude with a sharpened stick of charcoal. It was a moment of acute embarrassment, but only for a short time. Then the professor came into the studio. He was a precise little man with a thickly curled brown moustache, gold-rimmed spectacles and quiet voice, named W. Felton Brown. Without any preamble he strode up to the model, his right thumb extended, and with a sweeping gesture from her shoulder to her ankle, pointed out the "line of light and shade" that was the cornerstone of his teaching. His circle of docile draftsmen didn't catch it at first, but before many weeks the genius of his teaching began to seep through. A gentle, rather mysterious man, he took a fatherly interest in his students. More than two generations of MIT architects look back upon this gifted, kindly man with unforgetting affection.

Heading the School of Architecture at that time was the great Gothicist, Ralph Adams Cram, a dynamic man whose gifts as a speaker almost outshone his ability as an architect and writer. Once a week he gave an advanced course on the Philosophy of Architecture, and it became so famous that his classroom contained as many gate-crashing Boston Brahmins as students. Frequently I joined the un-invited listeners and sat entranced while this witty and erudite critic traced the history of architecture, accompanied by dull grey lantern slides that dated from the 1890's. They only served to emphasize the brilliance of the speaker.

In addition to such stern subjects as design and descriptive geometry, our class was given instruction in watercolor by Professor Harry Gardner, who also taught the classic Roman orders of architecture that his students adapted to stilted bank façades in later life. A part of our instruction was outdoor watercolor painting, and on Fridays we would repair to the Public Garden with pads of Whatman paper and collapsible sketch stools, and splash away with Windsor and Newton's best watercolor paints. These were my first artistic attempts, and it is just as well that they have vanished. The experience, however, proved to be of great help in later years.

Looming up in the future as the ultimate, the utterly sublime reward for architectural excellence, was that glamorous institution, the MIT Traveling Fellowship. The competition for this prize was the climax of the school year, and the talented winner received a year of travel abroad, expenses paid. Some advanced design students tried for Boston's Rotch Traveling Fellowship, and a few ventured into the fabulous company of aspirants to the Paris Prize or the topmost honor of all, four years of study at the American Academy in Rome. To me, the most exalted, the most deliriously desirable of all human attainments, was to win a fellowship for travel in Europe. The thought of rolling through France or Italy on a bicycle or in a third-class coach was totally utopian. Sketching in knickerbockers in an Italian village,

4

making rubbings with shoemaker's wax in an English churchyard, finishing measured drawings in an attic bedroom in Paris, these were incredibly adventurous ways of life. My lowly undergraduate state excluded me from the select group of aspirants to the prize, and the interruption of World War I meant that I never even entered a competition. In retrospect, however, it seems that much of my life has been an extended traveling fellowship, not just for a span of years but for a few decades. As such, it perhaps deserves further scrutiny.

In the next year, 1916, most of "Boston Tech" moved ceremoniously across the Charles River to Cambridge. The School of Architecture, however, remained in Boston and took possession of the original Rogers Building on Boylston Street. A classic brick and stone edifice, it was a credit to the Back Bay, only to give way later to a mastodonic insurance building. It is illustrated here by a drypoint that I made many years later.

Defence Turret of the
S.S. *La Touraine*

With a desperate war raging in Europe, the next year was not a tranquil one for undergraduates. Many New England students enrolled in the American Field Service, a group of volunteers who drove ambulances on the Western Front for French infantry divisions. The reports that they sent back glowed with adventure, and I became obsessed with the desire to drive a Ford on the Chemin des Dames. Private funds were needed, however, and my resources were far too slender. To solve this problem I was sent to interview no less a Boston dignitary than Colonel Henry Lee Higginson. The courtly white-haired gentleman received me sympathetically in his State Street office, heard my brief story, and instructed his secretary to provide me with a generous letter of credit on a Paris bank. He did this for dozens of college boys who needed help to join the ambulance corps.

Thus the way was cleared to embark on a traveling fellowship of a different sort, and on the second day of June, 1917, I was one of about two hundred and fifty collegians who crowded the venerable French liner *La Touraine* in New York. In my duffle bag were a camera, a box of watercolors and a small pad of Whatman's paper, and during the Atlantic crossing I made a wash drawing of the forward defense turret, with a gun manned by two French marines. Looking back on this breach of security, I am amazed that I was not thrown into the brig.

Porte du Palais, Bordeaux. This gateway facing the cobblestone quais of Bordeaux was sketched in later years.

After ten days the ship wound its way up the Gironde River early one morning, and through a porthole I had my first glimpse of France. Here were the gentle slopes of the Médoc, ribbed with ripening vines, and now and then a village of low white houses capped with rose-colored tile roofs radiant in the summer sun. Closely packed plane trees sheltered a river-front street of country stores and cafés, a scene of total tranquillity. That was enough for me. I became a Francophile on the spot, and have never ceased to have a deep affection for rural France.

A march along the cobblestone quais of Bordeaux to the railway station, an overnight train trip on the unyielding wooden benches in third-class compartments, and we were in Paris, somewhat disheveled but exhilarated by a first glimpse of that beautiful city. We had pre-

Café in Chambéry, watercolor painted on leave, September, 1917

Landscape near Meaux
Watercolor

ceded General Pershing and the first American troops to land in the capital by about ten days. For the ensuing fortnight we camped in tents in a fine old French garden in Passy, waiting to be assigned and getting fitted for uniforms. With whipcord trousers and belted, patch-pocketed jackets, we looked as much like British officers as we dared.

There was no time to make jottings in the sketchbook during these first exciting days in Paris, but soon the scene shifted. One of a contingent of replacement drivers, I was sent to a training camp in a rambling old flour mill near Meaux. Surrounded by patchwork fields of wheat and barley, it was the pure essence of France. The slopes were gentle, the red-roofed farmhouses clung close to the ground, and the hills were a paintable patchwork of golden yellow and soft green. My aspiring watercolors of that idyllic countryside were puerile, but at least they were fresh. I batted off a dozen of them before being assigned to Section 14 of the Field Service, composed of a flamboyant group of Stanford undergraduates. They served the 55th French Division in the Monts de Champagne sector, near Reims.

After this the sketchbook received scant attention. I managed to make a few watercolors of wrecked churches and farm gates in dreary little Champagne villages, but am much prouder of the fact that I helped pick the grapes of the 1917 vintage of Champagne, which was a good one. We were billeted in the vineyard-rich village of Villers-Marmery, and joined the grape pickers with enthusiasm.

It was in Section 14 of the American Field Service that I had my first taste of French cooking and wine. Our chef, Monsieur Lebec, was a chemist in civilian life, and *la bonne cuisine* came naturally to him. Out of several vegetables and dubious cuts of beef he fashioned a classic pot-au-feu that delighted the *ambulanciers. Poule au pot, navarin,* and once in a while a classic *boeuf à la mode* were other savory standbys, accompanied by great platters of *pommes frites.* Being with the French Army, we were entitled to half a liter of wine per day. The humble French *pinard* possessed no subtle bouquet, and it left a purple stain on the teeth. Still it was heartening for the morale.

Monsieur Lebec, the French chef, and Denhez, his assistant

Another great advantage of serving with the French Army was that we were entitled to the same *permission,* or leave, as the *poilus.* Approximately every three months we had the privilege of spending seven days, plus travel time, in a leave center, and before the war ended I had visited Paris, Nice, Dinard, Aix-les-Bains and Biarritz. A few ambitious sketches resulted from these trips. The life of an *ambulancier* was a busy one, however, and my portfolio of drawings from the war period is a slender one. There were more important things to be done, and I have always felt that I served a useful purpose by staying with my Ford ambulance throughout the war.

Following the armistice I wangled a job painting scenery for a doughboy musical comedy called "Let's Go." Deserting my comrades in a muddy village in the Argonne, I was transferred to the unaccustomed luxury of a heated room in Neuilly-sur-Seine, outside Paris, and worked happily on theatrical sets for weeks.

Then came the long wait for the trip back home. It included four weeks sloshing amidst the mud and duckboards at the notorious Pontanazen camp outside Brest. Finally an immense converted freighter crammed a few thousand of us on board and steamed out of Brest's dreary harbor. We had shed our muddy uniforms for new gear, including tin helmets and shiny hatchets, and the word got around that we were due to march triumphantly up Fifth Avenue. When the silhouette of our homeland appeared, however, it consisted not of Manhattan skyscrapers but the sandy Virginia shore off Newport News. My twenty-two months of overseas adventure ended on a rather subdued note on that day in April, 1919. An obscure Private First Class, I wore the Croix de Guerre, awarded after the Second Battle of the Marne.

The Author at Ste. Menehould, August, 1917

After demobilization at Camp Lewis, Washington, and a long vacation with my parents on the Pacific coast, it was decided that I should complete my architectural studies at MIT. I took the four-day train ride back to Boston in September, and was fortunate enough to join a group of some fifteen architectural students and draftsmen who had rented a four-story brick house at No. 9 Walnut Street, on Beacon Hill. It was a gifted gathering, including a fine pianist and several lesser musicians. A rented piano brightened up the *salon* which doubled as a drafting room, and soon proper young Boston ladies in lavender tweeds began coming for tea. Within easy walking distance were the

Perspective rendering of proposed Memorial in the
Charles River, Boston

Rendering of plan of proposed Memorial in the
Charles River, Boston

Gateway in the Oise

robust steaks at Durgin-Park's market eating place and the seafood delicacies of the Union Oyster House. It was a happy setting for the returning veteran.

The School of Architecture had been reduced to a handful of students during the war years, and seemed disorganized when we enrolled for the new term. Ralph Adams Cram had departed, and some weeks elapsed before the identity of the new Dean was disclosed. His name was William Emerson, and I will never forget the first time he greeted his students. Tall, thin and distinguished, he wore an architect's typical black moustache and the thin red ribbon of the French Legion of Honor in his buttonhole. Possessed of great poise and tact, he also was endowed with a warm sympathy for his fellowman, a sense of civic obligation, a modesty and a generosity that left an indelible imprint on two generations of students.

A direct descendent of William Emerson, the fighting parson of Concord, and a great-nephew of Ralph Waldo Emerson (on whose knee he recalled sitting), he brought immediate life and animation to the school. A graduate of the École des Beaux Arts in Paris, he was

8

superbly equipped as an educator, and his twenty years as Dean were accompanied by solid advances in the teaching of design. Some of today's foremost architects got their start under this warmhearted, perceptive man, and many of them became his friends for life. Although he graduated from Harvard the year I was born, we soon struck up a close friendship despite the disparity in our ages. It was based partly on our mutual affection for France and for sketching, but it went much deeper than that. He had a profound effect on my life, as later pages will show.

Unhappily, the routine of the drafting room began to pall on this returned doughboy. How to keep him busy with the T-square and triangle after he'd seen Paree was quite a problem. I began to drift away from architecture by writing would-be sophisticated songs for the Tech Show, and making pen-and-ink drawings for VooDoo, the college humorous paper. The plunge into commercial art was not far away. *House Beautiful* was located in Boston at that time, and soon I was making pen-and-ink pages of fireplaces, curtain valances and kitchen gadgets for its rather gushing lady editor. This led me to an advertising agency that wanted pictures of languorous ladies using bath salts. Down the precipitous path I went and learned the difficult art of drawing shoes that would be acceptable to the readers of the *Boot and Shoe Recorder*. Then I approached the Display Manager of Filene's with decorative window cards done in opaque watercolor, with a space for hand lettering. He agreed to take a dozen a week, and the die was cast. I called on Dean Emerson in his office in the Rogers Building and told him that I didn't want to be an architect after all. I was the first student to leave him, and sometimes I blush.

I find it convenient to forget the succeeding months as a commercial artist, mostly devoted to ignominious assignments—bookplates, pipe tobacco, lingerie, asbestos roofing. The only noteworthy venture I undertook was a set of color renderings for a Memorial to Soldiers, Sailors and Marines to be erected in the Charles River by the City of Boston. It was proposed to build an island on which would stand a lofty carillon, an open-air theater and two classic pavilions. Chandler Stearns made the plans and elevations in his room at our Walnut Street diggings, and I spent months working on the large and elaborate perspectives and plans, rendered in color. They were exhibited in the Boston Public Library, and this was about as far as this chimerical project ever got.

The wanderlust took hold after this, and for no particularly good reason I packed up and moved back to Seattle, where I made a round of the advertising agencies and was soon busily turning out commercial art on everything from mattresses to windshield wipers. It was dull stuff, but life was brightened by many old friends from the University of Washington, where I had spent two years. Months went by until one evening when I was dining in morose and solitary fashion in the Puss 'n Boots restaurant. Beside me was an opaque brownish glass partition, and silhouetted against it was a large rat foraging among the catsup bottles. Something snapped within me that instant, and I realized that this was not the life for me. Within a few days I had sold my

William Emerson at his summer home in Senlis

Périgueux

9

A Courtyard in Amboise

Fifteenth-century houses, Amboise

studio, converted my slender resources into traveler's checks and made a reservation to sail for France. My own private traveling fellowship was in the offing, and morale soared to Olympian heights as the Northern Pacific sped me eastward. At the French Line pier in New York lay the small ship *La Bourdonnais,* booked for a total of fourteen passengers. Never have I seen a more desirable vessel. A congenial fortnight at sea and I was in Paris, sitting at the Café des Deux Magots with a cluster of Beaux Arts students and breathing the heady elixir of life. It was mid-April in 1922, and the buds were already well out in the gardens of St. Germain-des-Prés across the way.

My stay in Paris was brief, only long enough to buy pencils, sketchbooks, watercolors and a collapsible sketch stool on the Rue Bonaparte. I crammed these in one large carry-all leather bag and took the train to the old château town of Amboise on the river Loire. The horse-drawn coach of the Hotel du Lion d'Or was waiting at the station. Clumping cheerfully across the bridge we drew up at a hospitable riverbank inn, where the landlord gave me a top-floor room with a view. That night I dined on *saumon de la Loire au beurre blanc* and half a bottle of Vouvray, and life never seemed better. The next morning I was out early and made my first timid pencil sketch. The traveling fellowship was on.

I stayed in Amboise about a fortnight, sketching earnestly in pencil but having more success with my watercolors. My pencil drawings were wiry little things that portrayed the architecture but not the values. I should have remembered to apply Felton Brown's line of light and shade to old French houses. One of my first discoveries was that a sidewalk sketcher leads an exposed life. Much of the time I was surrounded by schoolchildren in their black *tabliers,* and they were almost always impressed. The first exclamation was usually "C'est bath!" (That's swell), and after a pause the next remark would invariably be "Tu ne peux pas faire autant!" (You can't do as well). I heard both expressions for years. I liked the children (unless they sniffled) but felt less cordial to other uninhibited onlookers—town mongrels and village sots. On more than one occasion as I sketched an old house I was invited inside by the proud owner. After a glass of wine or two the conversation turned toward real estate, and without much subtlety I soon was being urged to buy the house. Sometimes it was difficult to convince them that my American accent didn't indicate a Texas fortune.

Sketching in a country town makes the artist a part of the community. I was welcomed in the best Amboise café and invited to join the *belote* players. Shopkeepers knew me when I stepped into their stores, and groups of pretty girls walking arm in arm along the mall gave me a smile during the evening promenade. I hated to leave the place.

A ride in a third-class compartment of a leisurely *omnibus* train took me to Loches, another château town filled with good sketch subjects—town gates, Gothic towers, a rambling château containing the tomb of a fascinating lady, Agnès Sorel, and a most forbidding dungeon. I visited the Town Hall in Loches looking for a *Carte*

The Cloister at Saint-Benoit

d'Identité, and was startled to find that the mayor was none other than a grizzled old stretcher bearer whom I had known during the war. He was more than cordial, and we repaired to the corner cafe for a reminiscent *petit verre.* The next day I was surprised to hear the town crier beating his drum at street corners and reading something from a slip of paper. It concerned "a *dessinateur américain,* Monsieur Chamberlain, who is honoring our city for a brief visit. Any courtesies that may be shown him will be appreciated by his Excellency, the Mayor." French hospitality assumes many forms!

After Loches I chugged over to Chinon, birthplace of Rabelais, and sought out its least expensive hotel, called the *Herse D'or* (Golden Harrow). My finances were strained, and I asked for a cheap room, which happened to be over a blacksmith shop. The next morning I awoke to inhale the penetrating fumes of scorching horses' hooves. The guttural oaths of the blacksmith arose at the same time. Some horses were only mildly obstreperous, and were merely cursed as a camel or a pig by the bellowing smithy. The more incorrigible horses received rougher epithets, however, and were cursed as cows or even chambermaids to a cow, the ultimate insult. I came to like the aromatic morning tirade, and kept the same bare room throughout my stay. It was in Chinon that I discovered that my sketches were negotiable for French currency. I struck up an acquaintance with Madame Tharraud who sold peasant lace in an outdoor stand by the château gates. She agreed to offer my matted sketches to American tourists on the basis of a fifty-fifty split. A benevolent lady from Buffalo bought six of them the first day, and I was enchanted. Now I wish that I had them back, for they were my best ones. Money soon arrived from home, and I peddled my wares no more.

Vieille Maison, Loches

The Dungeon, Loches

La Maison du Saumon, Chartres

Château Gaillard

The château country was irresistible, and I spent days in Blois, Langeais and Azay-le-Rideau before heading for less familiar provinces, the Anjou and the Poitou. Before the summer months whizzed by I had crisscrossed the country around Paris, depleted my funds but fattened my portfolio impressively. It contained literally hundreds of sketches and watercolors.

In September it was Chartres that beckoned. Here I joined two architectural colleagues from MIT and a quiet Yale graduate named Thomas in a small provincial hotel. Thomas told us of an intriguing assignment that awaited him. He had been named dramatic critic for a new magazine that some daring young Yale graduates were going to launch soon. Its name was to be *Time*.

Chartres was the climax of the summer, the high point of my "traveling fellowship." After an exciting week, it was time to repair to Paris and find an inexpensive ship bound for New York. I roomed in a small hotel on the Rue de Seine, haunted the bookstores and the French Line office, and finally obtained passage on one of their less imposing ships, the *Roussillon*. It was thronged with college students, and life on board was gay and unfettered. Everyone had a chance to get acquainted because the ship developed engine trouble, and on some days logged only about sixty miles. Under such favorable circumstances I came to know a comely New York girl of Scottish ancestry named Narcissa Gellatly. She had been serving with Anne

Sunday Morning on 57th Street, New York (1923)

The Plaza from Sixth Avenue, New York (1923)

Morgan's American Committee for Devastated France, and was so pretty that she was always selected to be photographed in uniform at the gateway of the Château de Blérancourt for publicity purposes. She spoke fluent French, showed a keen interest in art, and generally brightened the surroundings. When the ship arrived in New York I was glad that she lived in Washington Mews and not in Ashtabula.

New York was the next logical step, and I sought out an old university friend from Seattle to join me in finding a furnished apartment. His name was Leland Tolman, and one of his jobs with Dillon Read on Wall Street was to work with James V. Forrestal on financial statistics. He was brilliant and witty, a wordsmith and something of a dude, and proved to be an inspiring roommate. We found a large front room in a brownstone house on 57th Street, now replaced by Steinway Hall. The room was fairly well furnished, but the water ran far too slowly in the bathroom, and Leland constantly complained about "basting" himself in the tub.

The time had come to convert my fat collection of French drawings into tangible assets. I matted several dozens of them, put them in a clean portfolio, and began the round of the architectural magazines. Photography had not monopolized their pages at that time. The edi-

A Street in Romorantin
(from *The Century*, December, 1922)

13

Church of Saint-Etienne-du-Mont, Paris

tors were still interested in draftsmanship, and they were kind to my modest efforts. *Architecture* and *Arts and Decoration* ran portfolios of them, and so did the long departed *Century*. Richardson Wright, the magnetic personality who edited *House and Garden,* liked the drawings of French manor houses, and ran them in his magazine. I sought out H. I. Brock of the New York Times and he used my French sketches as fillers for the Book Review section for many weeks. Some of the drawings were rather affected, with puffy clouds and tapestried skies, but nobody seemed to mind. *The Architectural Record* commissioned me to make their covers, and *The American Architect* signed up for a series of illustrated articles. It was a gloriously busy winter with some outdoor sketching on Sundays and commercial art sandwiched in. One of my advertising assignments was to draw all the John Wanamaker buildings from 1823 to 1923, a project involving about 600 windows. They appeared in a double page spread in *Vogue* on January 1, 1923, and I used the proceeds to buy an engagement ring for the fair Miss Gellatly. She had consented to join me on my next traveling fellowship, due to begin in the spring. We were married in Grace Church in New York on a sunny day late in April, 1923 (a good wine year), and sailed for France the next morning on the French Line ship *Chicago.* Our assets justifying this bold voyage consisted of an American Field Service Scholarship and a magazine contract.

The venerable French ship enjoyed a tranquil spring crossing. Passengers were few but congenial. We sat at a long table presided over by the Commandant, and reveled in the honest French cooking and wine that we had missed so much in New York. After eight days the chalk cliffs of Le Havre loomed up, and a short train ride through Normandy took us to Paris and my cherished St. Germain-des-Prés quarter, where the Hotel Jacob et d'Angleterre was our home for this and many future sojourns in Paris. By dusk we were sitting on the terrace of the Café des Deux Magots with a group of fledgling American architects. Some were Paris Prize winners, among them Percival Goodman, John Ames of Boston, and a tall, smiling, angular fellow named Wallace K. Harrison. Surrounded by a chattering group of French students was the cleverest draftsman and most proficient prize winner of them all, Lloyd Morgan. More than anybody in the business he knew what influenced a jury of architectural judges, and later demonstrated this gift at Yale as a professor of design. Among the earlier generation of American Beaux Arts architects on the café terrace were Clarence Zantzinger, Julian Levy, and Ralph Walker, all fervent Francophiles. However, the personality who drew the greatest circle of admirers, both French and American, was a short greying man with a crewcut and an absolute mastery of French drafting room slang. He was Raymond Hood, destined to achieve fame as a master planner of Rockefeller Center. My responsive wife was bewildered but obviously impressed. That night she had a vivid nightmare in which it appeared that everybody in the whole world was an architect with a moustache, a toothy smile, and a tweed suit.

Within a few days I introduced her to the railway carriage and country hotel technique that I had perfected the year before. We took

Rue Grenier-sur-l'Eau, Paris

Le Coq Gaulois

Normandy Manor House at Canapville

Courtyard of the Hotel du Grand Cerf,
Les Andelys

the train to Chartres, which was an inspiration, of course. There is no better initiation into the spiritual beauty of France. After a few days we rolled along to a sketching pilgrimage in Dreux, and then to Les Andelys, where we stayed at the magnificent timbered Hotel du Grand Cerf and became lifelong friends of the owners, Albert Champsaur and his American-Canadian wife Gwynned Weller.

In Paris I had bought a watercolor box, some tubes of Lefranc colors, a block of Arches paper and a sketching stool for my new companion, and in Chartres I began to give her lessons in watercolor painting. She didn't need many, and proved to have a much better color sense than her teacher. After a train ride to Rouen we changed our means of transport and bought a second-hand open model-T Ford. This opened up a new horizon. We rolled unfettered through Normandy and on to the Champagne country to visit my wartime villages and drink a few toasts with my old French friends. Before the summer was over we had a perfectly wonderful outing, visiting cathedral towns such as Reims, Bourges and Tours, and batting out sketches with abandon. By October we were in the Basque country where we sold the Ford and took the train to Burgos, our first Spanish city. An exciting fortnight in Avila, Segovia, Madrid, Seville, Cordoba and Ronda, well punctuated with pen-and-ink sketches, and we were in Gibraltar, ready to board the freighter *Gibel Sarsar*. This small ship had a few cabins for passengers, but its main function was to crisscross the Mediterranean at night, spending each day unloading in a different port. It had a Dutch captain but sailed under the Union Jack, in token of which we had early morning tea, and later were served a delicious Indian curry with rice and chutney for breakfast. The nights were less pleasant, and very rough. From Melilla in Spanish North

A Street in Tunis

The Duomo, Florence (right)

Africa to Alicante the deck below swarmed with seasick grape pickers who wailed loudly until dawn. At Oran a cargo of half-dead cattle was unloaded by lassos that grabbed their horns in a cluster. We were happy to leave the ship at Algiers, in spite of that tasty morning curry. A train took us for stops of a few days in Constantine and Tunis, where I boldly, perhaps imprudently, made sketches in the bazaars. Then a steamer took us from Tunis to Palermo, and soon we were settled for a long stay in a snug hotel with a divine view—in Taormina.

Christmas in this lofty Sicilian village was gay and rather social, and we found several friends among the Anglo-American artists who made it their home. In February we took a train to Salerno and Naples, and then a car to the incomparable Amalfi for a long stay. Here I did an illustrated story about the Amalfi drive for *Travel* and splashed around with large-scale wash drawings. Rome had us intimidated. It seemed too vast for a brief visit, and we skipped it in favor of Florence

Symbol of Florence

17

Gaston Dorfinant at his press, with his wife, Céline (lithograph by Madame Carpentier)

The Rennaissance Loggia, Colmar

where we settled in one of those homelike pensions for which the city is famous. More wash drawings and pen-and-inks before we decided to return to Paris and see it again in the springtime, pausing in Avignon, Orange, and other sunsoaked cities long enough to fall in love with Provence.

We settled in a comfortable Left Bank hotel and I took a new tangent—lithography. A few of my Beaux-Arts friends had experimented with the medium, and one of them took me to the studio of a master lithographer, Gaston Dorfinant. His atelier was in the far end of a courtyard near Nôtre-Dame, on the Ile-de-la-Cité, and its broad windows overlooked the Seine. An utterly charming and unassuming man, Dorfinant wore an artist's broad-brimmed black hat and a high-buttoned tunic such as Monet might have worn. There were eight work tables in the studio, each equipped with a lithographic stone and a crescent-shaped wooden apron to protect the stone from fingerprints. Some of the tables were occupied by commercial draftsmen making letterheads or labels for strawberry preserves or shoe boxes. Others were reserved for book illustrators, poster artists or students like me. Some fascinating personalities sought out this friendly craftsman, and during my time there I came to know Luc-Albert Moreau, the illustrator, Vertès the gifted Viennese draftsman, Vlaminck, the vivid Belgian painter, illustrator and printmaker, and Mariette Lydis, creator of pensive and very beautiful portraits. They would finish their drawings here, and Gaston would then process the stone and pull impressions in an adjoining room. The atelier was a carefree and happy place, partly

The Sheltered Street, Vitré

Porte du Vieux Pont, Sospel

A Bay of San Marcos, Leon

A Moorish Gateway in Toledo

Unsymmetrical Doorway of the Convent
of Santa Maria, Salamanca

because of Monsieur Marcel Petitjean, the commercial artist, who knew a dozen operas by heart and would sing Madame Butterfly in a rich baritone voice complete at a single sitting.

The change from graphite pencils to wax lithographic crayons was simple, and I plunged into the new medium with enthusiasm, copying many of my old drawings on stone. Drawing them in reverse called for discipline, but Gaston had thought of everything. He provided a table mirror, and by looking at my drawing upside down in the mirror I had a good reverse image. Furthermore Gaston knew how to cater to the vanity of his customers. He would print their modest lithographs on luxurious Chinese paper, and sometimes embossed them with a plate mark fashioned from a cardboard mat. Again he would

Detail of the Town Gate,
Fuenterrabia

21

Rue de la Bucherie, Paris

*Vingt
Lithographies
ℨu
Vieux Paris*
par
SAMVEL CHAMBERLAIN

pull an *épreuve contrecollé* which consisted of a very thin moist sheet of buff or pale blue Japan paper that ran through the press next to a sized sheet of French stock. The result was a more colorful and luxurious print. You could have prints in two or more colors, if you wished, and Gaston furnished the instructions.

In the midst of all this excitement I received an offer from Charles Harris Whitaker, editor of the Journal of the American Institute of Architects, to undertake a series of architectural sketches of Spain. These were to be published as a portfolio, with an advance royalty guaranteed. I could see the fine hand of William Emerson behind this proposal, but could never verify my suspicions. We had a little family conference on this, and decided to cable my wife's mother to come to France and furnish companionship while I was touring about Spain. She obliged, and I went back to my swaying, rattling third-class rail-

Porte St. Martin, Paris

way coaches once again. The trip began in Gerona and before six weeks had elapsed I had done Tarragona, Zaragossa, Toledo, Avila, Segovia, Salamanca, Léon, Zamora, Burgos, and several intermediate stops. Spanish ironwork and complex sculptured detail were delineated this time, and I no longer hesitated to tackle a cathedral or a rich Gothic doorway. The portfolio was entitled *Sketches of Northern Spanish Architecture* and appeared later under the imprint of the Architectural Book Publishing Company. It was printed by the Meriden Gravure Company, printer of the volume you are now holding.

I returned to France to find my two ladies summering tranquilly at Beaugency on the Loire. They were staying at a pleasant country *auberge* with excellent food. The strawberries had never been bigger or more delicious, and the great stalks of white asparagus were irresistible in French dressing. But more important matters than gastronomy were pending, and in mid-June our first daughter, Narcisse, made her appearance at the American Hospital near Paris. She was a total success, and we proudly took her by taxi to a furnished apartment near the Parc Montsouris on the Left Bank. With the apartment came an enormous stroke of good fortune in the person of the cook and *bonne à tout faire*. She was Madame Francine Gauthier, a red-cheeked Burgundian who speedily indoctrinated us into the subtleties of French cooking. She stayed with us for years, and became the heroine of one of our books, *Clémentine in the Kitchen*.

A summer in the city gave me the opportunity to draw the Parisian scene as much as I wanted, and I embarked upon the idea of making

Maison de la Tourelle, Paris

23

Dome of the Church of the Val-de-Grace, Paris

Rue Saint-Séverin, Paris

Escutcheon in Granada

a portfolio of twenty lithographs of old Paris. I would set out on a streetcar daily with my sketch stool and grease crayons. It obviously wasn't practical to lug a heavy flat stone around on a wheelbarrow, so I compromised and drew on a sheet of zinc with a soapstone surface. At other times I used transfer paper that Gaston skillfully reproduced in reverse on his studio stone.

The subjects were varied, and scattered all over Paris, from the Porte Saint Martin on the crowded Grands Boulevards to the modest pewterer's shop in the Cour du Dragon, long since disappeared. The church of the Val-de-Grace adorned with scaffolding that had not been removed in twenty years proved to be a good subject, and so did the Maison de la Tourelle in the heart of the Marais. The twenty lithographs took all my patience, for the month of August turned out to be the rainiest in the annals of the weather bureau. Each morning I struck out bravely only to encounter rain, forcing me to wait disconsolately in a café for a change of weather. To me a certain melancholy attaches itself to the portfolio of *Vingt Lithographies du Vieux Paris,* even though they are cheerful and sunny. Gaston pulled a hundred prints of each subject and we bound them loose-leaf in a hundred

24

A Bridge in the *Basse-Ville,* Chartres

Bridge on the Quai Notre-Dame, Chalons-sur-Marne

natural linen portfolios, with each print numbered. Enough relatives and friends seemed to acquire them so that expenses were soon covered on my first publication, date 1924.

That summer William Emerson was in Paris busily organizing a very beautiful book called *Old Bridges of France.* The text was by his classmate at the École des Beaux-Arts, Georges Gromort. Dean Emerson commissioned his old *patron* at the École, Monsieur Victor Laloux, to write the preface, and the eminent watercolorist, Pierre Vignal, to make a series of watercolors of old bridges. Over forty exquisite measured drawings were made by an anonymous French draftsman. Finally the Dean asked Louis Rosenberg and me to travel around and portray specific old bridges in pencil and wash. We pursued separate paths, but both itinerant pencil pushers spent a few happy and fruitful weeks in the country.

In the fall the William Emersons sublet their Paris apartment to us. It was located at 23 rue Las Cases, and faced the church of Ste. Clothilde and a coquettish little park where stands the statue of César Franck. He had once been the church organist. Furnished with old French pieces and endowed with adequate plumbing, the apartment brightened the adventure of living in Paris. A small *salon* served as my studio. My morning walk took me along the rue St. Dominique where I used to see a neat little man with a flowing gray moustache, a double-breasted overcoat and a Homburg. Almost every man who passed him lifted his hat, and before long I realized that this was Maréchal Foch, on the way to his office in the War Ministry. Never have I seen a more modest warrior.

Pont Valentré, Cahors

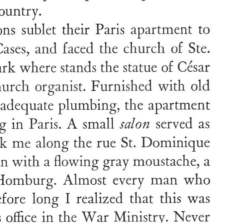

Gateway in Spain, Pencil Drawing

Gateway in Spain,
my fledgling attempt at etching

The logical step after lithography seemed to be etching, and I made a few do-it-yourself attempts with a zinc plate, following instructions in Lumsden's book. They weren't very encouraging, and again I asked one of my Beaux-Arts friends, Lansing ("Denny") Holden, where to find a good etching teacher. Denny knew just the man, was taking lessons with him, in fact. One eventful morning he led me to the studio of Monsieur Edouard Léon, located at 6 rue Vercingetorix. A long dank, typical Left Bank corridor led to the glassed-in ground floor atelier of the master, who was a cheerful, greying little man with a twinkle in his eye, and a good sprinkling of Paris *argot* in his speech. He was a graduate of the École des Beaux Arts and not only knew the technique of etching perfectly, but also how to impart it to others. After a tour of his atelier I could hardly wait to sign up for individual lessons, and agreed to take two a week for a stipend that even then seemed cheap.

There was no fooling around with Monsieur Léon. He meant business, and during my first lesson I learned to clean a copper plate thoroughly with benzine, vinegar, and whiting, then to apply an extremely thin coat of etching ground with a *tampon,* or pad. After that I smoked the surface of the plate with a wax taper and was panting to work on it with an etching needle when the lesson ended. Under his close instruction I learned to transfer the main lines of my model drawing in reverse on the blackened copper plate, then to needle the subject and to protect the back and the beveled edges of the plate with stopping-out varnish.

After that came the immersion in the acid bath, either in iron perchloride or nitric acid. Monsieur Léon had me make a trial plate with different etched areas subjected to different exposures under the acid, a guide to how deeply bitten a line would be after so many seconds or minutes in the acid bath. The whole thing was fascinating, even if my first few plates were rather pathetic. Plate printing came next, and my mentor demonstrated the technique—cleaning the newly etched copper plate, daubing it with etching ink, wiping it with coarse, crisp muslin, and finally hand wiping it and giving it a deft touch with a soft muslin called "retroussage" before cleaning the beveled edges and laying it on the clean steel bed of the etching press. Over it he laid a sheet of dampened Arches paper, adjusted the thick felt blankets on top of this, and slowly turned the wheel of his old-fashioned press. After the plate had passed under the roller came the breathless moment when the blankets were lifted and the freshly printed proof was delicately peeled from the plate. It is a moment that no etcher will forget.

As the weeks passed by Monsieur Léon taught me other facets of the etcher's art—how to handle a *burin,* the engraver's triangular steel wedge, and the sharpened steel needle of the drypoint specialist. By midwinter I was making softground etchings, using a soft, rather sticky ground that was mixed with mutton tallow. This was rolled on the plate and then smoked and unified with a wax taper. The plate was attached to a small drawing board with thumbtacks and on top of it was laid a piece of fine tissue and another sheet of thin drawing

The Fish Market, Chartres (soft ground etching)

paper. The drawing was then made on the upper sheet of paper, and everywhere the pencil touched the soft wax was lifted to the tissue paper. A hard pencil produced a thin line, but a soft pencil left a sketchy impression almost like charcoal. Once bitten in the acid you had a pencil drawing on copper, and a perfect foundation for an aquatint, which came next on the instruction schedule. Monsieur Léon taught me how to coat the plate with a powdering of resin, then to heat it with great care so that microscopic little apertures were left on the surface, and finally how to bite the plate in successive acid baths so that it was a tapestry of tones of varied intensities. This was the technique of the color print that had so many successful exponents in those days, T. F. Simon in particular.

Monsieur Léon encouraged me to use his etching press outside of lesson hours, and soon I was haunting his studio, pulling proofs of my newly etched plates. Some of them were a bit bombastic, showing the influence of Georges Gobo, a French etcher I admired greatly. My first published plate, "A Sidestreet in Beauvais," is one of these. Most of the others were quiet architectural studies of Paris street scenes, country churches, Gothic gateways in Spain, glimpses of Taormina, Amalfi and Florence.

My *patron* didn't point out their defects. Instead he encouraged me, along with his other pupils, to make up a framed group of my best

Amalfi

The Church at Sézanne

The Buttresses of Beauvais Cathedral

Gateway of Santa Maria, Burgos

prints and to enter them in the Paris Salon for 1925. We all complied, at considerable expense, and took our entries to the Grand Palais in a taxi. Monsieur Léon's influence with the jury seems indisputable, for my modest frame of three etchings won an Honorable Mention, and a paragraph in the Boston papers. He was intensely loyal to his students, who reciprocated by taking him to Paris restaurants and woodside picnics where the wine flowed freely, and the guest of honor showed great Gallic exuberance. In later years he had acquired so many worshipful ex-students in America that he made a special trip to our country and was wined and dined from New York to Texas. His pupils also arranged some successful one-man shows for him in American galleries. As an artist he excelled at watercolors and oils of Brittany, particularly of Roscoff, where he spent the summers. His etchings seemed a bit slapdash to some of us, but there was no question about his mastery as a teacher. Later I found that the best English instruction in etching technique had little that surpassed the ebullient master of the rue Vercingetorix.

A Sidestreet in Beauvais (first published print; First Honorable Mention, Paris Salon, 1925)

Old Houses in Ann Arbor (1926)

The Bridge at Pinos, Spain
(first attempt at drypoint)

My winter with him was prodigally productive, and by the following spring I had completed enough etchings, drypoints and lithographs to make a respectable one-man show. The pace was too rapid,
however, and some of those early plates weren't really qualified to be
hung in a gallery. So it was lucky that the idea of exhibiting was post-
poned. Instead, our little family packed up and sailed back to New
York on the *De Grasse*. We spent a few vacation weeks in Westport,
Connecticut, where the Gellatlys had moved, and where their first
grandchild made a memorable impression. I took my portfolio of
prints to Boston and showed them to Mr. Louis A. Holman of Goodspeed's Book Shop. This charming old-school Bostonian seemed to
like them when I called at the congenial shop on Park Street, and I
left a group of prints just in case they might like to exhibit them some
day. Two years later they did better than that. They offered to be my
American publishers, and served in that capacity for close to twenty
years.

In the meantime an unexpected offer came from the Middle West.
The head of the architectural school at the University of Michigan
had been reading my articles and decided to offer me a teaching post
at Ann Arbor. An assistant professorship paid a respectable stipend,
so September saw us established in a vibrant college community, indulging in a totally new way of life. Homeric football games before

The House of Monsieur le Curé, Mesnilles (Normandy)

80,000 spectators, fraternity dances and faculty teas, these entered our lives for the first time. My assignment was to teach second-year design, freehand drawing and outdoor sketching to an overly large group of students who were far more interested in mating than in architecture. I took the sketch class outdoors on several occasions, using a few sagging old Ann Arbor houses as subjects. Some of them proved adaptable to my drypoint needle. This was the twilight of prohibition, and I learned a good deal about student mores and "Canadian Port" before the college year ended. My most vivid memory, however, is of our little butterball of a daughter on a sled. No matter how carefully I pulled it, she would invariably roll off into the snow like a curled-up opossum.

Release to France couldn't come soon enough, and in early June we were back on the *De Grasse,* sailing with an unfettered crowd of college kids and vacationing professors. This time we spent only a short time in Paris to acquire a nasal Alsatian nursemaid, and then settled down in the Normandy hamlet of Bizy, on the outskirts of Vernon. We took two rooms over the pastry shop and restaurant of Monsieur Quervel, a gifted chef, who made the best *pâté en croute* and *poulet à la crème* in the region. His meals were simple, but absolutely delectable. Guests sat on a broad sheltered sidewalk terrace to sample his specialties and to watch the light traffic go by. We gazed in awe when

Old House in Westport, Connecticut (1926)

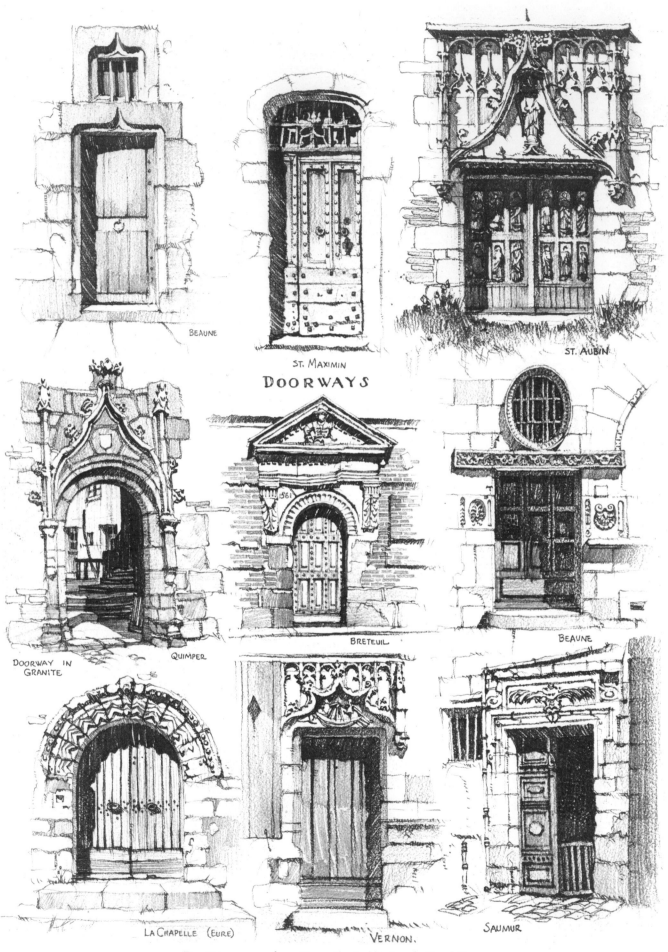

BEAUNE

ST. MAXIMIN

ST. AUBIN

DOORWAYS

DOORWAY IN
GRANITE

QUIMPER

BRETEUIL

BEAUNE

LA CHAPELLE (EURE)

VERNON.

SAUMUR

Doorways, a page from *Domestic Architecture in Rural France*

BRACKET FROM THE
AUBERGE DU VIEUX PUITS
PONT-AUDEMER

BRACKET IN NICE

WEATHER VANE FROM A
CHURCH IN THE OLD QUARTER
OF NICE

BRACKET IN
LaCROIX - ST. LEUFROY (EURE)

DETAIL
FROM THE ANCIENNE
DOUANE - COLMAR

DETAILS FROM THE ANCIENNE DOUANE - COLMAR

Metz
Freres

KEYSMITHS SHOP
SIGN IN COLMAR

FROM A WINDOW GRILLE IN COLMAR

SIGN ON A
PHARMACIST'S
SHOP IN COLMAR

SCATTERED
FRAGMENTS
OF
IRONWORK

ITALIAN
BRACKET FROM
AN ANTIQUE SHOP
IN MENTON

LANTERN BRACKET
IN JUMIEGES

DETAIL FROM JUMIEGES

DETAIL FROM Nº 20
RUE DES SAINTS PERES
PARIS

BRACKET FROM THE
MUSÉE SCHONGAUER - COLMAR

Scattered fragments of ironwork, a page from *Domestic Architecture in Rural France*

Hand-lettered title page of
Domestic Architecture in Rural France

The Market Place, Bourges, frontispiece of
Domestic Architecture in Rural France

Maurice Chevalier would appear on a Sunday fishing trip with a group of sophisticated, light-hearted and, to me, utterly sublime actresses from the capital. In fact, he was captivated by our daughter Narcisse, and presented her with a bag of *bon bons*. We came to Bizy because we had friends in the village, notably Dick Myers, Paris representative of the Curtis publications, and his wine-and-food-conscious wife, Alice Lee. They lived in a house on the hill, and in another small villa nearby was a quiet slender little couple who were totally preoccupied with writing and research. They had a Polish cook who prepared the meals and was scandalized when they sat down to the table, still glued to their books, and consumed their meals without a word to each other. She shouldn't have minded, for they were Rosemary and Stephen Vincent Benèt, who can be forgiven for anything. In his precise and disciplined manner, Benèt was writing *John Brown's Body* on this French hillside far from its American setting. Another author, somewhat more flamboyant, who lived at the Pension Quervel, was Charles Flandreau, author of the hilarious classic *Viva Mexico*.

This was a summer of endless outdoor sketching, for in New York before sailing I had arranged with Paul Wenzel, president of the Architectural Book Publishing Company, to prepare a book of sketches of French domestic architecture. We bought a little open Fiat "torpedo" with a round-nosed radiator and a shrill purr to its motor, and began a pen-and-pencil tour of the Normandy countryside. Some of these were large single-page drawings, but usually I placed three on a sheet, or else arranged a whole series of thumbnail sketches on a single page. Timbered houses, château farms, manor houses, thatched cottages, windmills, village shops and cafés, these were the favored subjects, but there were also details of doorways and gates, and drawings of wrought iron shop signs, latches and knockers. Before the summer had ended we had wandered far afield.

Our traveling fellowship was now a party of four, crammed with all our luggage into the Fiat. We sought out the most picturesque of all Normandy inns, The Auberge du Vieux Puits in Pont-Audemer, and enjoyed for a fortnight the seafood specialties and the *poulet à la Vallée d'Auge* for which it was famous. An ancient timbered well in the courtyard gave the Inn its name. On the façade hung a sign: "On Loge à Pied et à Cheval." The whole group of buildings made a superb sketch subject, and we both were busy with crayons and watercolors.

Sandy Calder joined us in Normandy about this time. He was equipped with a rickety bicycle, red wool knee-length socks, a wide black moustache and a loud penetrating laugh that rather startled the local townspeople. Still he loved Normandy food and Burgundy wine, and that turned the tide in his favor. France boasts of him now as one of its distinguished citizens.

Our next stop was a vacation hotel facing the sandy beach in a peaceful town called Arromanches. With my sketchbooks I roamed the countryside in Brittany while others relaxed on the placid Normandy sands. They weren't destined to be always so placid, for in June, 1944, Arromanches became the invasion beachhead known as Port Winston, and the whole town was blown to matchsticks.

34

Auberge du Vieux Puits, Pont Audemer

Pigeonnier at Boos, Normandy

Brittany was our next objective and we stopped in Vitré and Josselin before settling down for a long stay in a panoramic hotel in Dinan, one of the loveliest of Breton towns. The château of Vitré is an overwhelming affair, and I tried two lithographs of it on transfer paper. Our portfolios were getting fatter as we packed up once again and began the long trek to the Riviera. Through the Anjou, the Touraine and Burgundy we rolled, stopping for leisurely stays at modest country hotels. Living out of suitcases had its drawbacks, but it was a glorious trip. The roads were not cluttered with traffic as they are today. The pace was easy, the country hotels always seemed to have a place for us, and the rural gastronomy was inspiring. Our daughter became a *gourmette* at a very tender age, and it is not surprising that she is editing cookbooks today.

Antibes was our first stop on the Mediterranean. It was full of watercolor subjects, but we didn't care for the hotels, and moved on to Villefranche-sur-Mer, a seaport favored for generations by cruise ships and the American Navy. In the Hotel Welcome, a six-story hostelry overlooking the harbor, we found shelter for our little quartet, and spent most of the winter months there. We learned quite a lot about sailors, cruise passengers and Riviera personalities.

Two contrasting celebrities stayed for long periods in our hotel. One was Jean Cocteau, lean, long-fingered and poetic, who shared his quarters with a delectable little sunburned Parisienne at the time. In the dining room he amused himself by mocking the formal manners of the British guests, bowing to them in a solemn and deeply ceremonial manner. A fan-toothed young artist named Sir Francis Rose was also one of the guests, together with his mother and her ruddy-

The Porches, Dinan, Brittany

The Battered Boat, Villefranche-sur-Mer

A Mediterranean Acquaintance

faced gentleman companion from England. Their table in the dining room was usually the scene of tumult, as the older man could not abide the sight of the younger one, and made no secret of the fact. At one moment of alcoholic exuberance the white-haired Englishman made an attempt to amputate his own ear, but with less success than Van Gogh achieved. In contrast to these personalities was Hendrik Willem Van Loon, the Dutch historian, whose books achieved a phenomenal success in the Twenties. A large, hulking man with a sardonic sense of humor, he illustrated his own books with droll ink drawings, usually done with a match stick. I will not forget the day when he was surrounded in the hotel lounge by an adoring group of autograph seekers. They were schoolgirls from a cruise ship in the harbor, and one of them was bold enough to ask the master if he would make a drawing for them. Van Loon took out his ink bottle and match sticks and obliged by drawing his usual top hatted Dutch philosophers with long pipes. While the girls gazed eagerly over his shoulder he lettered out the appropriate motto: "A Dirty Mind Is A Perpetual Solace." They carried their prize back to the ship in slight perplexity.

An American cruiser lay at anchor in Villefranche for most of the winter, and we came to know a good many sailors. At first they

36

The Hilltop, Villefranche-sur-Mer (1927)

scurried to the bright lights of Nice some four miles away, but as the season wore on they frequented local waterfront bars. Most of them were quiet, homesick country boys, but a few were inclined to be belligerent after too many beers. They were good with their fists, but the little French sailors and waterfront characters had their own form of attack. With a jagged bottle neck as a weapon, they would slice and slash their adversaries, not deeply enough to be dangerous, but still inflicting long, bloody scratches. The shore patrol had its hands full on Saturday nights.

Villefranche and its precipitous streets were choked with sketch subjects, and I tackled them with everything I had—watercolor, pencil, drypoint, lithograph and dry-brush ink technique. With Clark Fay, a gifted magazine illustrator from Westport, Connecticut, I rented a bare room with a view of the harbor, and made it into a rather cheerful studio where we entertained our friends. Then the opportunity came to occupy a small villa in Menton, left vacant by my wife's aunt. So we moved a few miles eastward to this somnolent, somewhat smug and very picturesque old town on the Italian frontier for the early spring months. We loved the Riviera waterfront, the band concerts and especially marketing in the old quarter of the town. Menton has long been famous as a haven for artists, and the steep, ragged waterfront skyscrapers as well as the old harbor crowded with fishing boats proved

Old Menton (1927)

37

Skyscrapers of Menton

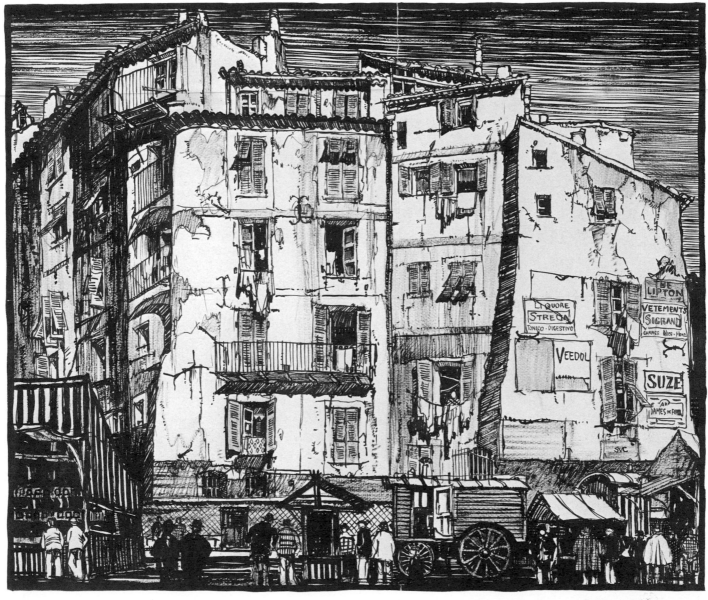

Carnival Time, Menton

to be irresistible sketch subjects. More drawings, drypoints and lithographs blossomed forth, some of which appeared in the architectural press.

While we had been in Ann Arbor, a gentle, bearded professor of medicine who liked etchings, Dr. Warren Lombard, told me of a scholarship for foreign study that had been recently established, and suggested that it might be just the thing for me. Without any particular optimism I sent in a package of matted prints and a rather perfunctory application for a scholarship to study etching at the Royal College of Art in London. Within a few weeks I had forgotten about it completely, and it was with a pleasant sense of shock that I opened a letter during our Riviera stay, sent by the John Simon Guggenheim Memorial Foundation in New York. They had accepted my application in their second annual list of scholarship awards.

This exciting turn of events foreshadowed an end to our gypsy-like existence. We decided to look for living quarters in Paris, something

The Quais, St. Tropez

Antique Shop, Boulevard Raspail, Paris

Entrance to the Cour du Dragon, Paris

that would be a good *pied à terre* while I led the student life in London. Late Spring saw our little Fiat spinning first to Aix-en-Provence and Avignon, then up the Rhone to Burgundy, and finally to Paris where we found a commodious studio apartment overlooking the Montparnasse cemetery. Before the summer was over I had finished the book of French sketches and drawn up a rather florid pen-and-ink cover and title page. As a frontispiece it carried an original etching of the marketplace in Bourges. It was published in 1928 by the Architectural Book Publishing Company, under the title of *Domestic Architecture in Rural France.*

So here we were in Paris in the midst of the Roaring Twenties, the era of F. Scott Fitzgerald, Ernest Hemingway and Gertrude Stein. We lived within a short stroll of the Dome and the Rotonde, and knew Foujita, Man Ray, Sylvia Beach and the famous model Kiki—all by sight only. One of the potentially famous persons we knew was Alexander Calder. He had worked in a lumber camp out in Washington near my home town of Aberdeen, and I knew him well. Even then he was inventing contraptions with wires and weights, and the loggers promptly labelled him "Goofy Al." Sandy's star was low on the horizon at this time in Paris, far removed from his triumphant one-man show that later occupied the entire Guggenheim Museum in New York.

This would be a good time for name dropping, but we can't claim to have been close to the greats of Montparnasse, even though we lived there. This didn't seem to be our *milieu,* and we were much happier in St. Germain-des-Prés, where the students from the Beaux-Arts held forth, and architects of several generations gathered. Here we developed a lasting friendship with R. Stephens Wright, a Harvard squash racquets champion, who had come to Paris to paint and later joined me as an etching student in the *atelier* of Monsieur Edouard Léon. With him was his slim, pretty sister, Brier, a singer of talent, and Alexander Stoller, a gifted sculptor, and later an amateur chef of great accomplishment. Through them we knew Aldous Huxley and his pretty Belgian wife, and Louis de Gielgud, brother of English actor John Gielgud. Louis' wife Mimi was a delightful Frenchwoman who became our lifelong friend. The whole group frequently met for an unfettered dinner party in a favorite Left Bank restaurant, where John Haldane, the British scientist, and his wife often joined us. We will always remember Haldane's vivid dissertation on the sex life of the snail, illustrated by flowing drawings on a marble-topped table. The Wrights even converted us to night clubbing, and before long I was accompanying Brier in Joe Zelli's nightspot, while she gave an emotional rendition of "Rain." It was a carefree moment, and life seemed the traditional bowl of cherries.

Our open Fiat could squeeze in six passengers, and almost every Sunday meant a *pique-nique à six,* a monumental outing in the forest of Senlis or Chantilly. This called for careful planning—visits first of all to the wine shop, then to the *charcuterie* for *pâté en croute, galantine,* and *saucisson à l'ail,* then the cheese store for choice Brie and Camembert, then the *boulangerie* for long thin loaves of bread, then the fruit store, and finally the *patisserie* for a cardboard box of choco-late eclairs, *madeleines* and *petits fours*. The hardier survivors of this feast usually played ball with little Narcisse for a time, and then every-one relaxed into a blissful doze.

Such an idyllic summer had to come to an end, and after another stay in Monsieur Quervel's hospitable inn at Bizy, and a sketching tour of Beauvais and Compiègne, we settled down in the large studio apart-ment on the rue Schoelcher. The faithful Francine came back to do the cooking, treating us to such established classics as *coquilles St. Jacques, filet de sole au vin blanc, boeuf Bourguignon,* and *gigot rôti* with white Soissons beans. A smiling youth from the Depot Nicolas kept us supplied with good, inexpensive red and white Burgundies. Friends dropped in almost every night for *café* and liqueurs, and life in Paris was assuming a charming pattern. It was something of a shock in early autumn to abandon all this for the uncertainties of an art school in London, and it was with slight misgivings that I took a taxi to the Gare du Nord and boarded the Golden Arrow.

"Pique-nique à six"

That night I had my first glimpse of London, and a decisive change it was. Instead of a commodious studio, I found myself in a top-story front room of a "residential club" on DeVere Gardens. It was com-fortable, and heat was furnished by a gas log in the fireplace, stoked by a shilling. The club was run by two imposingly respectable Scottish ladies, and the members were in the same category—retired colonels, semi-active businessmen and sedate greying widows. One always spoke in a subdued whisper in the lounge. Of one thing I was certain—there were no gourmets among the guests. Breakfast was British, and quite all right, but dinner offered a problem. The cook had a genius for mutilating good meat and fowl, and for drowning vegetables. A fine roasting chicken would come to the table in rags, and the "two veg" were waterlogged and tasteless. Still, nobody protested.

From a newly arrived student's point of view this was an exciting part of London. Albert Hall was close at hand, and the sprawling complex of London University, the Imperial Institute and the Natural History Museum lay along the footpath to my new school. The Royal College of Art occupied a rather gloomy side wing of the Victoria and Albert Museum. I sensed little of the buoyancy of the École des Beaux Arts as I climbed the grey stairway for my interview with the director, William Rothenstein. He was cordial, welcomed me into the fold, and told me of his esteem for other Americans who had studied etching here, Louis Rosenberg in particular.

Vieille Maison,
Rue St. Etienne-du-Mont, Paris

Within a few days I had met my fellow students, several of them girls, and all of them younger than I was, and the two instructors. Robert Austin, a very gifted engraver, was serious to the point of be-ing funereal, but Malcolm Osborne, R.A., head of the staff, was gentle and sympathetic. A handsome, white-haired Scot with a shy but friendly manner, he gained our confidence at once. A superb drafts-man, he was proficient in attacking a copper plate directly with a steel needle, and he had many fine drypoint portraits and landscapes to prove his skill.

Siena (first plate made at the Royal College of Art)

Gables of Colmar (drypoint made at the Royal College of Art)

When it came my turn to have a talk, he thumbed through my European sketches and finally selected a tall pencil drawing of Siena as a good drypoint subject. That was my first plate with him, and shows his influence. During the weeks that followed I learned the laborious process of "rocking" a mezzotint plate and creating an image with burnishers and scrapers. The technique of aquatint was somewhat more refined than what I had learned with Monsieur Léon, and I tried a two-color print with fair success. Robert Austin taught me some of the subtleties of the burin, but I learned most of all from a wonderful middle-aged Cockney whose name I have forgotten. He was in charge of the commissary that sold copper plates, paper, ink, wax, and many other things, and he knew as much about the technique of etching as anybody there. When the faculty was absent he would instruct the students in the art of cleaning and grounding a plate, biting it in acid and stopping out, and finally of printing it on dampened English paper. He taught me one of the most dextrous feats of all—how to flow a bath of liquid etching ground on a copper plate without leaving a flaw.

Plaza San Martin, Segovia (drypoint made at the Royal College of Art)

43

Hôpital St. Jean, Bruges (drypoint made at the Royal College of Art)

Malcolm Osborne encouraged his students to haunt the museums, the print shops and the auction rooms, and I was soon roaming through Colnaghi's, Sotheby's, and the British Museum on Saturdays. There was a good collection in the neighboring Victoria and Albert Museum also, and I had the privilege of leafing through fat solander boxes of Bone, Cameron, McBey and Griggs, the idols of the day.

One drawback of the school was that its working hours were short. An excess of leisure resulted. Being an eager beaver at that time, I spent many of the extra hours making drawings in the Victoria and Albert Museum, where nobody minded my collapsible sketching stool, pencils, and sketchpads. Ornamental ironwork from the Continent, English lead gutter pipes and Jacobean furniture seemed to be the most tempting subjects, and I set them down on a fine English rag paper especially suited to pen and ink. The architectural magazines in New York later printed them.

With all this leisure time on my hands I began to dig into the architectural library of the Victoria and Albert, casting about for a new book project. On the subject of Tudor architecture, my favorite theme, one superb book by Garner and Stratton had been produced decades earlier. The subject interested me enormously, and I thumbed through endless volumes to determine if any Tudor books had been done in recent years. None seemed to turn up, so I began to search out the

44

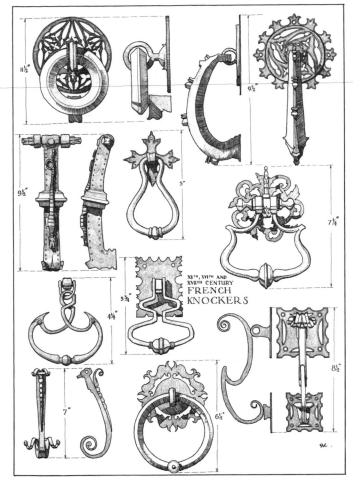

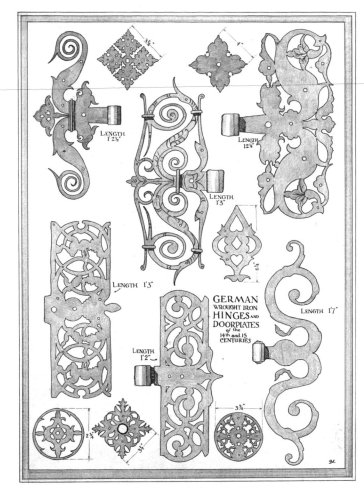

French Knockers German Wrought Iron Hinges and Doorplates

From the Victoria and Albert Museum, London

Tudor houses that Garner and Stratton had omitted. There were hundreds of them, and it was exciting work to evaluate them, pinpoint them on a map, and list them on a lengthy itinerary. I wrote to Paul Wenzel, the courtly old German-American publisher in New York, and his response to my idea was favorable, including a promise of generous advance royalties.

The winter was broken by a long vacation in Paris, but even so the stay in foggy London seemed long and a little melancholy. My good wife (hereafter known by her nickname, Biscuit) came over for *her* first glimpse of London, and that helped. We went to the theatre almost every night, dined at Rules and Verrey's and the Café Royal, and poked endlessly in bookshops. Two can enjoy London much better than one. How we missed the French cafés!

About this time I came to know a quiet and gracious authority on prints, Phyllis Dunthorne. Her father had established the Rembrandt Galleries of Robert Dunthorne and Son on Vigo street, and William Emerson had written her about my etchings. I brought down my portfolio one rainy day, and as a result she later asked to be my British publisher. Goodspeed's were already handling them in America, so I seemed to be in business. By April my scholarship at the Royal College of Art came to an end. I said goodbye to dear old Malcolm Osborne, but it merely should have been au revoir. After World War II we saw

Ironwork seen years later
in Italy

45

Cathedral Spires, Angers

him for a week or more in Chartres, accompanied by a young and very pretty wife. Their London home had been completely destroyed by bombs.

Paris seemed like paradise that spring, but I was not in a relaxed mood. My immediate problem was to get my etching and drypoint plates to a professional printer. The first step was to have my copper plates steel-faced by a specialist, Monsieur Knecht, who had a dank old workshop in the Marais. With great skill he would clean my plate, attach holders to the back, immerse it in a bath and turn on the electric current. The next day my plate would be coated with a microscopic film of steel, and ready to withstand the wear and tear of ink daubers, muslin rags and hand wiping. A drypoint plate thus protected was usually strong enough to yield a hundred good impressions, while an etching might run up into many more.

My plate printer was a sallow, cheerless man in his thirties named Edmond Rigal. He had a home and studio in suburban Fontenay-aux-Roses. He had spent years of apprenticeship in Paris before striking out on his own, and I was fortunate to be one of his first clients. He had the virtue of infinite patience, and would spend hours with me establishing a *bon à tirer,* or model print, for an edition of each plate. We would work on the highlights of each subject, on the sky value and the texture of the foreground. The test came in the hand wiping after the stiff tarleton rags had removed most of the surface ink. Edmond Rigal's educated palm could lay a smooth graduated sky that made my own veils of ink seem amateurish indeed, and he had the ability to pick out highlights and lay ink washes that came only from long experience. He was meticulous in wiping the bevel edge clean with whiting, so that it carried no tone on the paper. To recompense him for so much time and effort, I usually ordered a full edition of either seventy-five or a hundred prints. Often these were printed on a sensitive white Rives stock, but we experimented with fine Chinese and Japanese papers as well.

The opportunity to use ancient French paper for etching was also mine, for a few book and print dealers in open air *boutiques* along the banks of the Seine sold old eighteenth-century registers and account books. The front pages of these books would be filled with penned entries, but later the book would find its way to the attic, leaving a variable number of pages unfilled. These empty pages sometimes ran to a hundred or more. The bookdealers combed Paris attics for them, as they were most negotiable. This was pure rag paper, and superb for printing etchings. The pages often carried a decorative watermark, and usually were numbered in ink on the upper corner by a notary public. This was to prevent a furtive bookkeeper from tearing out a sheet. Above all, old French paper was desirable for its color. After a century or so it often turned to a delicate gray-green that led the French to call it "papier verdâtre." Meryon used this ancient paper for many of his etchings, and it was employed by several of the French masters of engraving of the nineteenth century. By haunting the *boutiques* I finally acquired a good stock of the precious old paper, and Rigal used it with happy results.

46

Long Wittenham, pencil drawing from *Tudor Homes of England*

Having set up the etching program, the next item on my agenda was to organize the trip to England in search of Tudor mansions. The book was conceived as a departure from its two predecessors on Spain and France. It was to be illustrated by photographs, pencil sketches and measured drawings rendered in pen-and-ink. This was too big an order for me alone, and I hoped to recruit a skilled architectural drafts-man to make the measured drawings. There was only one place to search out such a collaborator—the Café des Deux Magots. Among the familiar faces from the Beaux Arts I found an old friend from MIT. He was a slender fellow with dark piercing eyes and a neat waxed moustache, and his name was Louis Skidmore. He, too, was innocu-lated with a fever for architectural travel, and he seemed quite ready to join my expedition. Within a week or so we had everything or-ganized—tickets, visas for our passport and elaborate documents for the Fiat. Dean Emerson had provided an impressive letter of recom-mendation with a red seal attached, and the advance royalty from the publisher had been converted into traveler's checks.

Everything had been arranged for little Narcisse to stay in Paris with the nurse. So one May morning the three of us, Biscuit, Skid and I,

Title page, 1929

Broad Street, Ludlow: drypoint reproduced in *Tudor Homes of England*

Horham Hall, Essex

crossed the Channel with the energetic little Fiat and embarked on a new adventure. The plan was to take an easy motor trip from Southampton to a country hotel where I had made reservations for the night. Unhappily we encountered "customs formalities" and were so delayed that we reached our destination a few minutes after eight in the evening. It might as well have been midnight. Not a bite of anything was available in the hotel until we bribed the barmaid to bring us pressed beef sandwiches and three pints of Guinness. That taught us to be punctual about meal hours in the months ahead.

English summers can be rainy and disastrous, but 1928 was kind to us. We rolled about in the little open car, and rarely had to put up the canvas top. Sunshine was the order of the day, and my camera clicked merrily while Skid made notes with his metal tape measure and Biscuit batted off her fresh watercolors. My camera was a postcard-size handheld Kodak, using roll film, and not really up to the job. The pictures were sufficiently well-composed, but not as sharp as if they had been taken with a view camera on a tripod, with a black cloth sheltering the photographer.

48

Cottage at West Hendred, from *Tudor Homes of England*

My itinerary had blocked out a series of visits to manor houses and stately homes scattered over much of southern England. This meant that one of us would have to ring the bell at the gatehouse or the front door, and be confronted by a frosty and supercilious butler. Skid and I both were what is known as chicken in filling this role, and we gladly left the task to Biscuit, who had the gift of forthright speech and a charming smile. Once past the butler, the owner of the estate invariably proved to be utterly charming, and the soul of hospitality. Before the summer was over we had been invited to tea many times, and even to luncheon and dinner. Not only were we sometimes invited to spend the night, we stayed a long weekend with one cordial host, the owner of Gifford's Hall in Suffolk, and had a glorious time. We could write quite an essay on British hospitality!

Biscuit returned to Paris in late June, and we had to ring our own doorbells after that. We covered much more than stately homes during the summer. Cottages, farmhouses, old abbeys, wayside inns and almshouses all seemed fitting subjects. We sought out some of the most famous English villages—Finchingfield, Kersey, Chilham and Lavenham, and stayed in notable inns. At the Lygon Arms in Broadway we sketched and measured industriously in addition to rejoicing in the good food and wine. In the celebrated timbered Feathers Hotel in Ludlow we made drawings of the rich paneled interiors and struck up a rather forlorn friendship with a comely barmaid. I made a drypoint

The City Cross, Winchester, from *Tudor Homes of England*

Sunday Morning Sketch in Stanton

Cottage near Ashford, Kent,
from *Tudor Homes of England*

of Broad Street in this charming town, working with the copper plate on my knees and causing a faint stir of curiosity among the pedestrians. Three other drypoints, one of a Canterbury street scene, another of a stable court in Saffron Walden, and the third of the Founder's Tower of Magdalen College in Oxford were also drawn in this same direct manner.

We liked the Cotswolds best of all. Skid made copious notes and measurements of the old stone houses, and I tackled them freehand in pencil. At only one time was I acutely embarrassed while sketching in England. This was in the Cotswold village of Stanton where I was drawing a street scene of time-stained old Tudor houses. It was Sunday morning, and as the congregation left the church I found myself surrounded by an atmosphere of withering disapproval. One indignant parishioner stopped, turned to her companion and exclaimed "*Must* he do this on Sunday?" "I'm afraid there is no way we can stop him!" was the reply. I weathered the storm, but my ears were burning.

We lingered in England until September before closing our notebooks and portfolios and steering the little Fiat to Dover, and then from Calais to Paris. The homecoming at the rue Schoelcher was joy-

50

ful, and Francine had prepared a beautiful Burgundian dinner. Little Narcisse was more voluble in French than ever (with gestures) and Biscuit had been painting at the Académie Julien and attending André L'Hôte's classes.

As for Skid, he settled down with a drawing board in his Left Bank hotel room and began to finish up his measured drawings in pen-and-ink. I turned the remainder of the advance royalties over to him to help out with his expenses. This permitted him to spend a few extra months in Paris, during which time he met an attractive young art student named Eloise Owings. This set off something of a chain reaction. First of all, the two young people were married. Then Skid met his new brother-in-law, Nathaniel Owings, also an architect. Then came the Chicago World's Fair, where Skid acted as a sort of architectural overlord. Then the firm of Skidmore, Owings and Merrill made its debut. The meteoric rise of this establishment is known to all. Louis Skidmore in a few short years rose to the peak of his profession, receiving the Gold Medal of the American Institute of Architects, the highest award obtainable in this country. I've always thought it fortunate that some of that advance royalty was left over!

Our book was published by the Architectural Book Publishing Company in 1929 under the title of *Tudor Homes of England*. I made a hand-lettered title page and provided as a frontispiece an original etching of the Butter Cross in Winchester. Skid contributed thirty-one measured drawings, most of them reproduced in line cuts. Fifty-six of my pencil drawings and drypoints were printed on deckle-edge paper by The Meriden Gravure Company and tipped into the main body of the book. More than two hundred photographs were reproduced in halftone on a heavy, ivory-toned coated stock.

Founder's Tower, Magdalen College,
Oxford

With a rather lengthy introductory text, illustrated by sketches, this book was my most ambitious effort to date, and I went to New York to put it together. A single room in the Hotel Shelton, priced then at $3 per day, served as a workshop, and a fortnight elapsed before a complete dummy of this large volume, size 16 by 12¼, was ready. Each page had a layout, every picture had a final dimension and title, and space for all captions was calculated. Laying out a book is a marvellous way for an author to make a lot of extra work for himself, and I've been doing it ever since.

Of course, this has great advantages. An author can create the style and appearance of his own book, within limits, and the publisher is freed from the bother and expense of hiring a book designer. Since all of my subsequent books depended heavily on illustration and layout, it was gratifying to "write my own ticket" in the matter of book design, and my publishers came to expect it.

The Almshouses, Corsham,
from *Tudor Homes of England*

The same year Robert McBride and Company published *Through France with a Sketchbook*, rewritten from a series of my articles that had appeared in "The American Architect." This was something of a lighthearted travelogue with chapters on Normandy close-ups, Breton silhouettes, the chateau country, Riviera hilltops, toy towns of Alsace, a gastronomic promenade in Burgundy and an illustrator's angle of Paris. Its dull red binding looked like that of a fifth grade geography,

Cour du Marché, Bruges

Harness Shop,
from *Through France with a Sketchbook*

but it had a pleasant dust jacket showing old fishing boats in Étretat.

With over fifty etchings, drypoints and lithographs ready to seek their way in the world of prints, this seemed the right time to make a trip back to America and sound out the etching market. Edmond Rigal had an imposing collection of fresh prints for me to number and sign and, hopefully, to sell. About this time I was elected to the Société de la Gravure Originale en Noir, and we attended the annual banquet and initiation with Monsieur and Madame Edouard Léon. The cover for the menu was an original etching by Arthur W. Heintzelman, and I met him that night for the first time. A few days later Marcel Guiot, the well-known print dealer on the rue Volnay, signed up as my Paris publisher. Things were moving right along.

The chill of a Paris autumn was setting in as we packed our belongings, vacated the furnished apartment on the rue Schoelcher and took the boat train to Le Havre where the faithful *De Grasse* once again was waiting to take us to New York. There at the dock we were met by Biscuit's mother and father. They had moved to Twin Lanes Farm, a pleasant rural estate in Greenfield Hill, Connecticut, and their excitement at seeing their grandchild again knew no bounds. Little Narcisse smiled prettily, but she was openly vexed because nobody spoke French. "Ah, que tout le monde est bête ici!" she protested, and began to pick up her first fragments of English from the colored cook.

Greenfield Hill had a particular interest for me, since John and Dorothy Arms lived near the village green, and the Louis Rosenbergs were only a short distance away in Fairfield. We visited them both, and I spent a good deal of time in John's remarkable studio adjoining his old Colonial house. He invited me to go through his amazing library of books on printmaking, and assured me that he had read every one of them, usually on the commuter's train to New York. His vast collection of prints by other etchers was equally impressive. I doubt if any American printmaker has ever exchanged as many prints with his fellow artists.

With my family safely ensconced in the country, I went to Boston to visit my new print publishers. In charge of the print department at Goodspeed's was a soft-spoken young man named Charles D. Childs. He had taken matters right in hand, and had written a little monograph, bound in green boards, entitled "Samuel Chamberlain, Etcher and Lithographer." It was illustrated by a dozen black and white cuts, and contained an accurate list of my prints to date, some 64 of them. Furthermore he had arranged a series of exhibitions, the first to be held in Goodspeed's attractive gallery at 7 Ashburton Place. Others were scheduled for Cleveland, Detroit and Chicago, with a show in the Schwartz Galleries in New York last on the list. In most of these cities I gave either a lecture or a demonstration in the gallery, sometimes needling a small plate in drypoint, or printing impressions if an etching press happened to be available. These little affairs seemed to please the audiences, and the sales of my prints were encouraging.

William Emerson commissioned me to undertake a short series of talks on pencil draftsmanship and the graphic arts at the School of Architecture at MIT, and this proved most agreeable. My classes con-

Boston Fish Pier, 1929

sisted of advanced and graduate students who were genuinely interested in the refinements of pencil pushing. The editors of the Technology Review requested me to make architectural sketches of MIT
for its covers, and the Iconographic Society asked me to make a drypoint of the Tontine Crescent in Franklin Place, Boston, designed by
Charles Bulfinch and long since disappeared.

The profession of etching seemed almost Utopian in the spring of
1929, a charmed moment when everything appeared to be going well,
with no financial clouds on the horizon. We returned to Paris and
settled into the scene once again. Several American printmakers
flourished in France at this time. Arthur Heintzelman was celebrated
for his portraits, but the others concentrated on the French scene.
Robert Logan and A. C. Webb worked mainly on Paris subjects. Louis
Orr made very large, minutely etched plates that found high favor
with the French; some of his best were purchased by the Louvre and
reprinted in popular calcographic editions. Frank and Caroline Arm-
ington gave teas to members of the American Women's Club and
sold their etchings with sprightly success. Frederick G. Hall made
classic architectural prints while Cadwalader Washburn, a charming
and gentle Philadelphian with the handicap of being a deaf mute,
made beautiful drypoint portraits.

My formal debut in the Paris art world was made in May, 1929, at

The Tontine Crescent, Franklin Place, Boston

53

Sailors Home From the Sea, Étretat

The Curving Canyon, New York

the Galerie Simonson. In company with Maurice Achener, a courtly Frenchman of the old school, and José Pedro Gil, a talented Spaniard, I joined in an exhibition of etchings, drypoints and sketches. Señor Gil had the very best Spanish connections, and the opening of our exhibition was held under the "présidence de S.A.R. l'Infante Eulalia de Bourbon," the sister of King Alfonso of Spain. We can never forget that opening day. Little Narcisse had been attired in her best blue coat with a white fur collar, and given a large bouquet of roses to present to the royal lady. Before a beaming international audience she advanced with her bouquet, pierced her finger on a thorn, and barely averted a flood of tears as she almost flung her bouquet at the Infanta, who gave her a reassuring kiss. The exhibition was a success, as I recall it. At least we had some good press reviews. The *"supplément artistique"* of the Figaro gave us a most complimentary full-page review with three illustrations. There was, of course, a slight formality about paying the critic for his pains, but that was the standard operating procedure of the day.

Summer on the Normandy shore had long been our dream, and at last it seemed within our reach. We found a comfortable villa at Étretat, persuaded the loyal Francine to join us as our cook, and em-

54

Salamanca Cathedral, 1929

Drizzly Morning in Chicago

La Charité-sur-Loire

barked upon a most successful summer. One nice thing about the dry-point medium is that it doesn't call for an elaborate installation. A table, a chair, a good north light, and you have the essentials. Add a slight wooden frame covered with tracing paper to act as a reflector, and a mirror that shows your drawing in reverse, and you are in business. I claimed a small room at the end of the villa and made it my studio for about three months.

First I embarked on a series of drypoints of American subjects that Goodspeed's had undertaken to publish. Two of them were made from sketches of Boston—Faneuil Hall and the Fish Pier. Others depicted the canyon-like streets of New York, the skyscrapers of Chicago, and a glimpse of a Far West junk shop. Goodspeed's found a ready market for them at this affluent moment. A Spanish sketch of Salamanca was transferred into my first cathedral drypoint, and Rigal printed much of the edition on a beautiful blue-green French paper.

Early autumn found us in Paris again, where we took a pleasant apartment on the rue de Lisbonne, near the Parc Monceau. In addition to Francine we acquired a *femme de chambre,* one of whose duties was to take little Narcisse to school. On her first day at the École Deiterlein she sat on a rather high chair with her feet dangling in mid-air and was put to work with a steel writing pen and a bottle of purple ink. Over and over again on the quadrilled paper she made her *pleins* and *déliés,* full and fine up-and-down strokes of the pen. When she returned from her first day at school her light blue *tablier* was generously dotted with purple spots, and her fingers were like blackberries. But she was radiant. In the afternoon the maid took her to the Parc Monceau where she played with well-dressed, well-mannered French children, and enjoyed her afternoon *goûter.*

56

Verneuil

Cathedral of Sens

This was a felicitous moment for all of us. Filled with optimism and high purpose I embarked upon my largest plate to date, a drypoint of the magnificent Gothic tower at Verneuil, in central Normandy. It had taken me a full week to make the sketch the preceeding summer. It shimmered with Gothic detail, a superb subject for an architectural print. A few years later, John Taylor Arms, with his extraordinary courtesy and consideration, actually wrote me and asked my consent so that he could etch the same subject. That wasn't necessary, of course, and John made his etching at almost the same scale as mine. The only difference was that he did not reverse his etching on the copper plate, and as a result his print is in reverse, while mine adheres to nature. I will have more to say of this amazing and warm-hearted man in later pages.

About this time Steve Wright and I found a studio in an unbeautiful part of Paris facing the Prison de la Santé. It wasn't inspiring, but we had an etching press, and a wood stove to combat the cold. We worked there most of the autumn and winter, but my most vivid recollection has nothing to do with etching. Rather it concerns the most famous gastronome in Paris, named Curnonsky. We were in the habit of taking lunch at the Restaurant Couteau nearby, an unassuming place with exceptionally fine food. One day we sat at a table next to a portly man with a napkin in his collar and a carafe of red St. Jean-de-Braye in an ice bucket beside him. This is one of the few red wines in the world that should be chilled. If our neighbor had been Rembrandt I couldn't have been more excited. The greatest of all French epicures, he almost never paid for a meal, and rarely dined at mid-day. When he did, he chose the simple splendor of the Restaurant Couteau, and paid his bill. Before the winter was over I had a speaking acquaintance with the old gentleman. However, he was convinced that all Americans were Coca Cola-guzzling barbarians, and I never obtained the gastronomic story that I was longing to write. Years later I finally did write my story. It was a tribute, and an obituary, to the crusty old gourmet, published in the *Altantic Monthly*.

The stock market crash in October, 1929, should have been a warning, but it was nothing of the sort. We had often dreamed of finding a little old French house in the country and remodeling it for contemporary living. This seemed to be a good time. We had friends, the Karl Cates, who owned an ancient house in the old-world town of Senlis, some forty kilometers north of Paris, and we often drove out there on Sundays, vaguely looking for the ideal little manor house. After casting about for a few Sundays we surprisingly came upon an old house that came close to our dream. It was a conventional limestone house whose rather severe shuttered street façade gave only an inkling of the architectural joys beyond. The garden elevation, in the true French manner, was a thing of unfettered beauty, filled with gayety and light. It was a simple two-story façade five windows wide, capped by a faded red tile roof. There were two gardens on different levels, and a magnificent tree furnished a benevolent shadow in one corner. Senlis was once a fortified town and this property on the rue du Temple, fenced in with high stone walls, sloped toward the ancient

Our old house on the Rue du Temple, Senlis

bastions. There was a utility wing that could be transformed into a laundry, a garage and a studio. It all seemed highly desirable, and we tried to conceal our enthusiasm when we entered into negotiations with the owner, a cautious, oily little man, eager to extract the maximum from the sale. After a few weeks of whittling and maneuvering, we met before Monsieur Louat, the notary (who also happened to be the mayor) and signed the sales agreement, an impressive document on legal paper, bedecked with expensive French stamps.

Soon we were deeply involved in remodeling the old house, and had acquired a mason, plumber, carpenter and heating expert. Two new bathrooms, a modern kitchen, new dormers, and a maid's room in the attic, these were some of our extravagances, along with central heating. We made weekly inspection trips from Paris, usually stopping at the Flea Market at St. Ouen on the way back to seek out some old French furniture. This was a golden moment to furnish the house with antique pieces, for the Flea Market offered any amount of Provincial furniture, Louis XV and Louis XVI commodes, armchairs, *bergères,* and tables, at prices that today seem ridiculously cheap. By this time we had a new and larger Fiat "torpedo" and with its top down it could transport an *armoire,* a secretary, or a refectory table without straining. Our Sundays were usually orgies of spending at the ragged old furniture mart, and of transporting our prizes back to Senlis. Oaken stools for choir boys, a barber's chair with an adjustable back, stone mortars, Louis XIII side tables, marble-topped chests, all these were a part of the plunder—anything, in fact, except beds. We wanted new, insect-proof beds.

Towers of Senlis

Market Day in Lillebonne

Dentelles Gothiques, Clamecy

Silhouette of Senlis

College St. Vincent, Senlis

Week days during that long Paris winter were less frivolous, and I spent most of my time working on Gothic drypoint subjects. "La Charité-sur-Loire" was a street view of the great Benedictine abbey with its awkward duncecap tower cut off at the top of the plate. "Market Day in Lillebonne" showed a slender Gothic tower surrounded by timbered houses and the animation of an open air market. The architecture of the tower left something to be desired, and I tried to distract the viewer's attention by rendering an idyllic French sky with my ruby needles. "Dentelles Gothiques," the most ambitious Gothic plate that I ever attempted, was finished in February, 1930, and took me over a month. This amazingly complex example of late Gothic lacework comes from the west façade of the Church of Saint-Martin in Clamecy, an inspiring hill town just west of Burgundy. Nothing could be richer than the finely carved doorway, the rose window and the flying buttresses. It was a severe challenge to my presumptuous steel needles. The next month I finished the façade of the "Cathédrale de Sens," and a large plate of the rather shabby and delightful "Skyscrapers of Menton." It was a productive winter, and I kept my suburban printer, Edmond Rigal, in a turmoil of activity.

Meanwhile the work of the leisurely entrepreneurs in Senlis dragged on for months, and we were in a frenzy of impatience. Finally in May

62

we left the Paris apartment and moved to a furnished cottage in Chamant, on the outskirts of Senlis, where we could be close to our prize. The next month we literally pushed the painter out of the house and installed ourselves, with the faithful Francine occupying a new room with running water on the attic floor. It was a glorious moment —our very own house for the first time, furnished with Flea Market antiques, endowed with American creature comforts, and blessed with fine Burgundian cooking.

The Mason's House, Senlis

We were especially proud of our *salon,* which reflected the contemporary French influence. Its walls were of freshly scraped cream limestone from neighboring quarries, and dark red tiles covered the floor. Bookcases flanked the modern fireplace, also framed in limestone, and a wall of mirrors ran from the bookcases to the ceiling. At the focal point of the room we placed a large and very handsome painting of a reclining nude by our neighbor, Clark Fay. A large engraving by Decaris, portraying an undraped Andalusian belle, occupied another wall, and some realistic African sculpture in wood added to the *décor.*

It was about this time that our daughter Narcisse, who had been taught to read English by my mother, became captivated by the works of Louisa May Alcott. With great enthusiasm she read *Little Women, Little Men,* and *Jo's Boys,* among others. Years later she told us that she had mentally pictured all the interior scenes described in these books as unfolding in a stone-walled *salon* with nudes on the wall and primitive African sentinels on the mantlepiece.

The French residents of this conservative northern French town didn't exactly crush us to their bosom. It takes time to be received at the hearth of a French family, and often it never occurs. So we were happy that a small American colony was scattered over Senlis. John Ridgely Carter, head of Morgan and Company, lived in an aristocratic *manoir* near the old Roman arena, and his descendents still do. Hans Kindler, the cellist who became the director of the Washington Symphony Orchestra, and Karl Cate, a Bostonian who represented American firms in Paris for decades, both lived in our quarter. Best of all, we found a furnished house nearby for our beloved William Emersons, and they spent the summers there for several years. During one happy winter, our close friends, the Donald Moffats from Brookline, occupied this house with their family of vigorous schoolgirls.

Midsummer Silhouette, Senlis

Down by the little River Nonette was a rambling old house that appeared to be a remodeled mill. It had gardens on both sides of the placid river, an irresistible setting for a tall, sandy-haired American author who had a passion for flowers and gardening. His name was Louis Bromfield, and in a few short months he made his garden into the show place of the Oise. Sunday motorists gathered on the little bridge across the river and gaped in ecstasy. Louis Bromfield's technique as an author was to dig in his garden by day and meditate on the plots and characters of his current fiction. Late in the day he would repair to an upstairs room and dictate to his secretary, George Hawkins, who, with a name like that, was three-quarters Italian. The dictating chore being finished, the whole family would join at a large table in the kitchen and enjoy what the cook had prepared, or what they chose to cook up for themselves.

Fruit Store Façade, Senlis

Place Notre-Dame, Senlis

During the week, life was usually quiet at the Bromfields. Two of their three little daughters went dutifully to the École Nôtre Dame de la Victoire (as did little Narcisse), and the fiction ground out steadily in the upper room. But on Sunday the old house on the Nonette became a madhouse, the setting of a flamboyant garden party attended by all the available celebrities in Paris. They came down in droves, for Louis would ask them right and left, and invite them to bring their friends. The kitchen staff was instructed to be ready to serve from twenty-five to a hundred luncheons, and George Hawkins doubled as a proficient bartender. Mary Bromfield tried valiantly to keep up with the pace, which was dazzling. A typical Sunday influx of guests might include the Maharani of Baroda, Gloria Swanson, Gertrude Stein and Alice B. Toklas, Leslie Howard, Ina Claire, Edna Ferber and Helen Wills, the tennis star. Such a miscellany of exotic people kept the place in a gentle ferment. They stayed late into Sunday night, and incidentally furnished Louis with plenty of material for his next novel.

Our French friends were no less interesting. One was Charles Hallo, an illustrator of books, poster artist, and in recent years a designer of Hermès scarves. He loved the forest, *la chasse,* and everything that had to do with hunting, and was responsible for the Musée de la Vénerie, the hunting museum, in Senlis. We became good friends, and I often went to see him in his high-ceilinged, underheated studio overlooking a garden. The ledge outside his studio window was the favorite parade ground for a small flock of white, fantailed pigeons. Monsieur Hallo's remarks upon the morals of these "least pure of birds" were not complimentary. We saw this remarkable old man, well up in his eighties, less than two years ago in Paris. He still is illustrating books and designing Hermès scarves, and continues to join us for a good Paris dinner now and then. But we are not yet on a first-name basis after close to forty years. He calls me "Sham-bear-lan" and I call him "Mon cher vieux," and so it remains. Formality in France is sometimes deep-rooted.

Another friend was Madame de Bellegarde, an erect, distinguished and witty widow with a black velvet neckpiece and a salon filled with impeccable French antiques. What we recall most vividly about her, however, was her enormous wild boar. She had rescued the animal from the forest when it was tiny, and had raised him as a pet. Not entirely beautiful, he was friendly, and enchanted our little girls. Unfortunately he got his tusks entangled in a French door, and in trying to escape nearly pulled both of them out.

When we appeared in Senlis in 1938, before the outbreak of the war, Madame de Bellegarde invited us to dinner, a magnificent meal with a fine *filet de boeuf* and rare red Burgundies. There was a prophetic look of sadness in her eyes, and we never saw her again.

The literary light of Senlis was the Baron de Maricourt, an aging aristocrat who spent his mornings in bed, and formally received his visitors in a Louis XV bedroom. Asked about the state of his health, his reply was always the same: "Hélas, Madame, je n'ai pas de santé!" ("Alas, Madam, I *have* no health.") But his literary output continued, and his bedroom conferences were well attended.

Senlis from a Crow's Nest

Manoir d'Huleux, near Senlis

Ancien Hotel-Dieu, St. Leu d'Esserant

Early in our Senlis stay, Mrs. Bernard Carter, the banker's wife, came to me with an unusual request. Her son Shirley and her daughter Mildred (Mimi) were behind in their algebra, and needed coaching. "After all, you went to MIT, and you *must* know algebra" was her argument. You can't let your Alma Mater down in a situation like this, and I agreed to help them with their algebra at the large table in my studio. Shirley was about twelve, I would imagine, and his sister perhaps two years older. They came down dutifully with their notebooks, but seemed totally impervious to equations. Instead they stared at the etchings and watercolors that covered my studio walls, and wanted to know how they were made. I told them a little about outdoor sketching, and that was enough. More than anything else, they wanted to acquire some watercolors, blocks of paper, outdoor easels and sketch stools, and get to work. With their parent's consent, we embarked on watercolor expeditions on the outskirts of Senlis, with happy results. We tackled old bridges, country churches and shabby manor houses on many a sunny morning. My two junior pupils showed immediate talent, and went right on from there. In the years that have ensued, Mimi has given several successful one-man shows in

66

New York, while Shirley, presumably slated to be a banker, turned out to be nothing of the sort. For many years he has been a member of the faculty of the Parsons School of Art in New York, and has given several well-applauded shows himself. Plainly enough, algebra as well as geometry has its tangents.

The exhilaration of living in a country town gave me the impetus to try more drypoints direct from nature, and I made about eight of them during the summer months. The copper plate would rest on a small drawing board on my knees and the blue sky would reflect on the plate so that my drypoint lines were easily visible. By rubbing in a harmless paste of lamp black and vaseline, I could see the value of each line accurately. It was hard, exacting work, but usually rewarding, and most of the resultant drypoints were fresh and uninhibited. In the autumn I roamed the countryside in search of manor houses and made oversized drawings of them in Conté crayon. Biscuit perpetrated some corking watercolors, and life seemed bright indeed, especially as a newcomer was scheduled to brighten the family picture during the winter months. She arrived punctually on February eighteenth and assumed the name of Stephanie. A smiling new Swiss nurse was waiting when we returned with her from the American Hospital in Neuilly-sur-Seine. Beyond a doubt she was the prettiest baby of the year.

On my weekly trips to Edmond Rigal's studio I met many interesting French etchers, but one of them was outstanding. He was an athletic little man with very broad shoulders and narrow hips, and he wore his thick hair brushed forward like a Roman senator. This was Albert Decaris, the youngest man ever to win the Prix de Rome, the highest artistic award in France. His engraving at the École des Beaux-Arts won him the prize when he was eighteen, and his picture was on the front pages of the Paris papers the next morning. His four years in Rome were phenomenal, and he returned to Paris with a wealth of dramatic, oversized engravings, etchings and wash drawings rendered in India ink. I was struck by the overpowering scale and intensity of his work, which compared well with the best of Frank Brangwyn. His mastery of the burin was astounding, and I saw him at work in his studio on the rue de Seine. His copper plate was fastened to a large sloping drawing board that rotated on a swivel. In front of him hanging from a clothesline were his preliminary drawings, hung up in reverse against a strong light. Working visually from them, this dextrous man plowed through the copper with his steel burin, rotating the board when he required a curving line. The furrows of copper left his burin with a musical ping and fell to the floor. His speed was prodigious, as well as his accuracy. I bought a few of his large, silvery engravings, and was so impressed that I offered to approach Goodspeed in Boston, and Kennedy in New York, proposing one-man shows for this brilliant Prix de Rome. Both dealers accepted, and Decaris made his American debut in 1930, accompanied by excellent press reviews.

We became good friends of the artist and his attractive auburn-haired wife. On one occasion, which I will never forget, we stopped

Toledo, engraving by Decaris

The Andalusian, engraving by Decaris

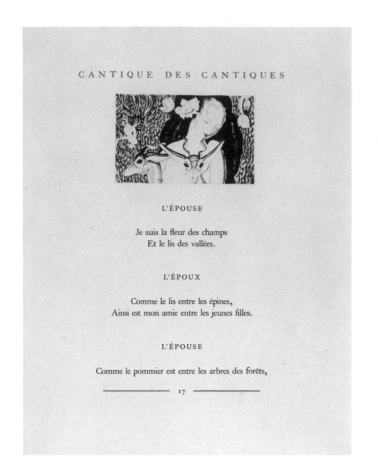

L'ÉPOUSE

Je suis la fleur des champs
Et le lis des vallées.

L'ÉPOUX

Comme le lis entre les épines,
Ainsi est mon amie entre les jeunes filles.

L'ÉPOUSE

Comme le pommier est entre les arbres des forêts,

——————— 17 ———————

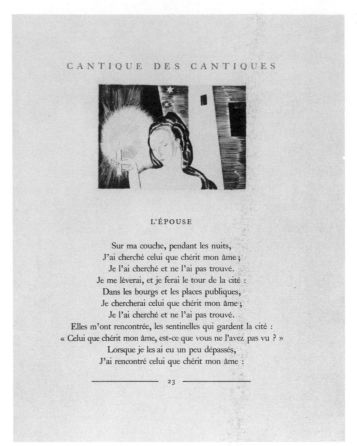

L'ÉPOUSE

Sur ma couche, pendant les nuits,
J'ai cherché celui que chérit mon âme ;
Je l'ai cherché et ne l'ai pas trouvé.
Je me lèverai, et je ferai le tour de la cité :
Dans les bourgs et les places publiques,
Je chercherai celui que chérit mon âme ;
Je l'ai cherché et ne l'ai pas trouvé.
Elles m'ont rencontrée, les sentinelles qui gardent la cité :
« Celui que chérit mon âme, est-ce que vous ne l'avez pas vu ? »
Lorsque je les ai eu un peu dépassés,
J'ai rencontré celui que chérit mon âme :

——————— 23 ———————

Pages from *The Song of Solomon* illustrated by Clark Fay (page size 10 by 13 inches)

Doorway of the Church at Le Thor

to visit them on our way to Senlis. On the floor in the back of the Fiat were two *langoustes,* roaming at will, which we had picked up at a fish market. Madame Decaris observed, with a giggle, that perhaps the langoustes might "faire pipi" on the car's carpet. At this her husband drew himself up and delivered himself of a sentence which seemed to us then, as now, a classic of style only possible in the French language: *"Une langouste, ma chère, ne se permet pas des fantaisies pareilles."* ("A langouste, my dear, does not permit herself of such fantasies.")

In the succeeding years Decaris carved a pre-eminent place for himself as a book illustrator. His work was invariably brilliant and dramatic. Later he changed from oversized impressions to very small ones, and designed many beautiful postage stamps for the French government. Today he is a member of the Institut de France and one of the great engravers of his generation.

Another artist who re-entered our lives about this time was Clark Fay, a talented American illustrator who had recently moved to nearby Chamant. He had studied with Harvey Dunn and N. C. Wyeth in New York, and was an old hand at illustrating the short stories and serials that appeared in *The Delineator, Collier's,* and *The Saturday Evening Post.* With three active boys, Clark had his financial problems, only partially resolved by his illustrations. We had known him in Westport, Connecticut, and on the Riviera and I greatly admired his

The Verdant Village, Bellefontaine

La Charité-sur-Loire

facility. Clark had his ambitions, and one of them was to illustrate a deluxe edition of that beautiful section of the Bible known as *The Song of Solomon*. I asked him if he felt ready to pick up the art of drypoint, in order to achieve such an ambitious project. Clark really didn't need many lessons in the medium. I lent him a few copper plates, some ruby, diamond and steel needles, and he was off. His first efforts were so lovely that I was bold enough to offer to be the financier and publisher of the new publication.

Within the next few weeks I had purchased the rights for the French text by the Abbés Glaire et Vigouroux, and had engaged Maurice Darantière, one of the most expert of French typographers, to set up the book and print it.

Monsieur Darantière was a rare book designer as well as a printer, and produced many small *de luxe* volumes, printed on exquisite paper and illustrated by original etchings by outstanding French artists. They have become collectors' items today, and are quoted at exalted prices in the catalogues. We were equally impressed by Darantière's typesetter, a stolid and handsome Swiss named Kayser. Without knowing a word of English he had set by hand the complete text of James Joyce's *Ulysses* and the proofreaders were able to detect only four errors.

Edmond Rigal undertook to print the drypoints, all of which were etched on copper plates larger than page size, so that no plate mark would appear. Clark's illustrations included delicate chapter headings

Chartres Cathedral, pencil drawing

Chartres Cathedral, first state, showing
basic outline made with ruby point

Porte St. Guillaume, Chartres

and tailpieces, and six full-page figure drawings. Almost all of them
were superb, although here and there the drypoint texture was a little
heavy.

Published in 1930 as *Cantique des Cantiques,* it was limited to one
hundred and five copies. Number 1 was printed on old French *papier
vergé ancien* and contained a folder with all the original drawings, and
the first states. Despite its ambitious price, it was snapped up at once
by a Paris collector. There were ten copies printed on old Japan paper,
and the rest appeared on French Montval stock. All of them were sold
within a year or so, and I suppose my publishing venture must be considered a success. However, it appears to have been my last.

The first pinch of the depression was evident in the months after *la
petite Stephanie* joined our household. Etching sales began to taper
off, and the bills from the entrepreneurs seemed to be rather unreason-
able. Still, this was no moment to let down. In my little studio in the
annex I began two ambitious cathedral plates. One of them was made
from a pencil drawing of the west front of Chartres that had taken
more than a week, and a great deal of neck stretching, to put on paper.
This subject is a bit austere, perhaps, and not the warmest interpretation of the beauty of Chartres. Yet there is no other way to show the

70

Chartres Cathedral, second state showing
unfinished texture on South Tower

Chartres Cathedral, final state

majesty of the two towers, one late Gothic, the other early Romanesque, and its divine rose window and portals. Years later I gave the
original drawing to the Boston Public Library. "Beauvais" was an extremely detailed drypoint of the south portal of this stupendous cathedral, whose nave is the loftiest in Christendom. The Gothic detail was
just as minute as my eyes could stand, and it took days to delineate the
lacelike portal. Adjoining the cathedral is the twin-towered Prefecture
of the Oise. This is standing today, but the buildings on the left and
the whole area back of them were leveled in World War II.

These were springtime studio plates, but in the summer I embarked
on a few outdoor subjects, etched with the drypoint needle direct from
nature. "The Verdant Village," a sylvan subject in the hamlet of Bellefontaine, is one of these. To me it is the essence of France, and it is
my favorite choice as a wedding present. (Perhaps you hadn't thought
of it, but an etcher *never* has to buy a wedding present, only a frame
for his chosen print.) "The Saplings" was a woodland scene, and "The
Abbey Farm" a fragment of ancient architecture that Griggs would
have liked. "The Country Road" was a rural landscape on a side road
near Senlis. Late in the fall I climbed several times to the top of the
church of St. Pierre at Senlis and made a drawing of the Cathedral of

St. Fargeau

71

The Country Road

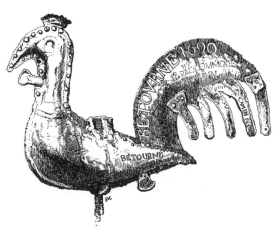

The Weathercock from Senlis Cathedral

Notre Dame and its adjoining gardens. It was published in November 1931 as "Senlis from a Crow's Nest," and gave me a fondness for climbing church spires. Some time later a scaffolding was erected on the Gothic south tower of Senlis cathedral, and I climbed it to make a bird's-eye view in the opposite direction, showing the disaffected church of St. Pierre, which served as the Senlis food market. The small area in front of the church was crowded with canvas-topped vegetable stands, and it made a dramatic, if somewhat busy, sketch. This was later made into a drypoint which was selected as the presentation print for the Society of American Etchers in 1939.

While the scaffolding was still in place, the town was shocked by the mysterious theft of the rooster that served as the weather vane. It was a heavy bird of lead and copper, but somehow the thieves made away with it during the night, and Senlis made the front page in the Paris papers. Later the rooster was recovered in the little river Nonette, and displayed in the cathedral garden, where I made a pen-and-ink sketch of it. Replacing the *coq* on his lofty perch called for a proper ceremony, and I joined my friend Monsieur Hallo and other town

72

Beauvais

dignitaries who laboriously climbed to the top level of scaffolding. Here the heavy bird, newly patched and riveted, was restored to his proud position with a fitting blessing by the *Monseigneur*. Then everyone descended to the fine old mansion that served as his residence, and participated in a *Vin d'Honneur*. It was another of those little occasions that one never forgets.

Thanks to William Emerson, a further opportunity to travel presented itself about this time. He had embarked upon a new architectural book with his old *Beaux Arts atelier* companion, Georges Gromort. The subject was French brickwork, a rich theme that lent itself well to pencil drawing. Fine examples of brick chateaux and manoirs flourish in Normandy, the Touraine and the Berri. Superb tapestry

73

Pigeonnier at Bouchou, from *The Use of Brick in French Architecture*

Château de Chapeau, from *The Use of Brick in French Architecture*

Château de Fleurigny

brickwork is found in Burgundy, and in parts of the Midi almost everything from dovecotes to cathedrals is built of large square pinkish bricks.

It was a rare assignment for a pencil draftsman with the wanderlust, and during a two-year period, with the family safely installed in Senlis, I embarked on several sketching trips to the brick-rich regions of France, and a little expedition to Belgium as well. These were not timid sketches such as had appeared in Dean Emerson's bridge book. More decisive and on a larger format, they portrayed the scale of the brickwork with broad pencil strokes of varied intensities. At least six grades of pencil were used on such drawings. They were the most ambitious ones that I had ever attempted, and the dean appeared pleased.

With printing costs climbing, it seemed prudent to print the brick book in separate paperbound volumes, the first of which appeared in 1935 as *The Use of Brick in French Architecture*. The splendor of Albi cathedral dominated the book, but the smaller subjects—town gates, parish churches, forgotten chateaux and windmills, doorways and covered wells—had a more intimate appeal.

Five other volumes, dealing with central France, Normandy, Ile-de-France, Flanders and modern French brickwork were scheduled to

Romorantin

Bruges in Belgium

Hotel Payre de Brens, Gaillac,
from *The Use of Brick in French Architecture*

The Town Gate, Lescure, from *The Use
of Brick in French Architecture*

appear. Unfortunately the first volume on the Midi encountered a tepid reception among architects still smarting from the depression, and Dean Emerson abandoned the rest of his project. In later years he generously returned my drawings that he had commissioned.

Living in a home of our own instead of a rented apartment or a hotel room meant that at last I could indulge my yearning for books. Tempting bookshelves had been installed in the salon of our Senlis house, and there was no longer a valid reason to hold back. Book collecting can become a bankrupting passion if it is not controlled, and I decided that the most enjoyable solution would be to specialize. The subject that interested me most was gastronomy—food, wine and fine cooking—and I decided to concentrate on that. Visits to old Paris bookshops produced early treasures at very fair prices—volumes by Carême, Grimod de la Reynière, Bauvilliers, Gouffé and Montagné, many of them autographed. Our Burgundian cook, Francine, was not interested in them, but she took kindly to more modest volumes by Edouard de Pomiane, and especially to *La Bonne Cuisine* by Madame E. Saint-Ange. The collecting bug bit me severely, and I have never recovered. I am always poking through catalogues in search of some treasure that may have been missed. In Italy, London, provincial France and here

76

MANOIR DE BAIS

Manoir de Bais, Normandy

Quai des Rosaires, Bruges

General Washington Saying Farewell to
His Officers in Fraunces Tavern, New York

at home I have gradually acquired a library of over 1,200 volumes on gastronomy. It is a lasting joy and a priceless source of information and recipes for the epicurean books that the two of us have written in recent years.

As the months swept by, the depression had an intensifying effect on expatriate American artists. My revenues were slumping, and the problems of being a homeowner in France were mounting. In such a situation, I was particularly happy to receive a letter from John Arms, inviting me to become one of twenty American etchers to undertake a portfolio of etchings portraying twenty significant episodes in the life of George Washington. This bold and unprecedented project had the backing of Arthur H. Brook, and the sponsorship of the Yale University Press. They had wisely selected John Taylor Arms to be the inspirational force, the catalytic agent, father confessor and imploring coach for this amazing venture. Some of the selected etchers, particularly those who were also illustrators, easily produced fine, free, spontaneous plates that were a joy to behold. Dear old George Wright made a superb print, and so did Kerr Eby. Some of the landscape and architectural printmakers who were selected had more of a problem, and I was one of these.

My subject was George Washington saying goodbye to his generals in Fraunce's Tavern in New York after the end of the Revolutionary War. A wealth of documentation was sent to me, including portraits of all the principals, exact details of their uniforms, and a plan of the room in which this touching event had occurred. It was a rare opportunity, accompanied by a respectable stipend, and I gave it everything I had. Unfortunately an etcher trained in architecture lacks a certain facility in portraying General Knox in tight-fitting white trousers clasping the hand of his commander in chief. I managed to make those trousers glisten in the late afternoon sun, but there was something wooden in the facial expressions of these eminent military men, and I wasn't very happy about my final result. When the portfolio finally appeared I was consoled to find that I was not the only etcher to be given a subject inappropriate to his talents. But John Arms was heroic to the end, and sent me a richly worded congratulatory letter.

Harkness Tower, Yale University,
preliminary sketch for etching

Once this plate was finished, it seemed only fair to allow the Gellatlys to become acquainted with Stephanie, their newest granddaughter. So we closed the Senlis house and sailed back to New York. A hospitable roof awaited us in Greenfield Hill, but problems faced the family breadwinner. My first move was to approach Yale University through my new friend, Mr. Brook. He introduced me to a tall, aristocratic, auburn-haired gentleman who is known to generations of Yale men, George Parmly Day. He was treasurer of Yale University, president of the Yale University Press, and also the brother of Clarence Day, who wrote that American classic *Life with Father*.

I took a portfolio of my Gothic drypoints to New Haven and spent an hour in Mr. Day's office trying to point out how well Harkness Tower and the handsome mass of the Sheffield buildings and the rich Gothic portal of the library would look, once they were portrayed in etching. My dignified interlocutor took me to Mory's for lunch, and during this pleasant interval I volunteered to make a series of preliminary sketches of a dozen Yale subjects that might be suitable for etchings. The next few weeks were spent most pleasantly driving back and forth from Greenfield Hill to New Haven, and making pen-and-wash drawings of the Georgian and Gothic buildings that made up the Yale community at that time. The Yale boys were almost exemplary in those days—they all wore jackets and ties. Only their once-white buckskin shoes, grimy with age and mistreatment, foreshadowed the sartorial anarchy of today. Carl Lohmann, secretary of the University, and Mr. Day served as a jury of two to pass on my sketches, and things went swimmingly. Soon I was at work on detailed drawings, and by May final approval was forthcoming.

Davenport College, Yale University,
preliminary sketch for etching

During this same springtime I went to New York to see Kenneth Reid, my old classmate at MIT, who had become the editor of *Pencil Points*. This sprightly architectural magazine was dedicated to the draftsman as well as the practicing architect, and my pencil drawings had frequently appeared in its pages. Ken Reid was receptive to new ideas for a magazine cover, and I designed a layout with hand letter-

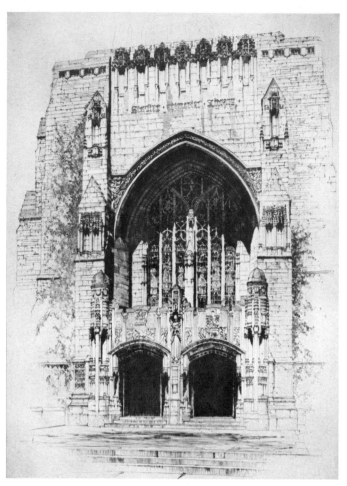

Sterling Memorial Library, Yale University

Sheffield Scientific School, Yale University

Pierson College, Yale University

ing at the bottom of the sheet and a bold square drawing at the top. The drawings for the first year were made with square Conté crayons, brownish red in color, and extended to three sides of the cover. A novel and vigorous technique resulted from these square crayons, which could be used both for sharp lines and wide tonal values. Any striking architectural subject seemed to be acceptable, and I was happy with the assignment, which lasted four years through 1936.

With Yale and *Pencil Points* standing behind us, we lost no time in sailing back to France. Joyfully we opened up the old stone house in Senlis, and called back the faithful Francine to the kitchen. This was a full summer indeed, and I wore down many a drypoint needle portraying the Gothic and Georgian splendor of Yale. One of the best subjects was the courtyard of Jonathan Edwards College with the Harkness Tower looming up in the background. Another was the flamboyant Gothic court of the Graduate School. But the "Colonial" subjects proved surprisingly good, especially the fine Georgian tower of Pierson College. The Divinity School, set on a hill far from the Yard, made a charming New England print.

Once a week I spent the day with Edmond Rigal, the etching printer, in his suburban studio. The depression had begun to hit him, too, and we were mutually grateful to Yale. We chose a variety of papers, French, Japanese and Chinese, to print up one hundred and

80

Jonathan Edwards College, Yale University

The Divinity School, Yale University

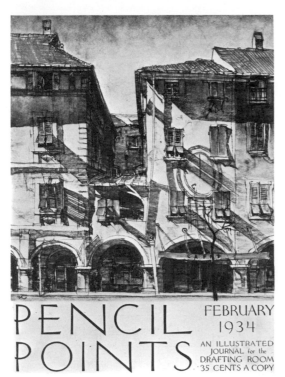

Pencil Points cover, February, 1934

twenty-five impressions of each plate. In some instances we were able to print up an entire edition of one plate on old French papers that I had picked up along the bookstalls on the Seine. Our Yale friends approved each model print by mail before Rigal started the edition. He was busy for months, with two lads to help him. *Twelve Etchings of Yale* finally appeared in a dark-blue linen portfolio in 1934, well publicized by the Yale University Press. The price was indisputably high, but loyal and affluent Yale men apparently are not hard to find. Many of them bought the portfolio for themselves, while others had each print framed and sent as a gift to their favorite preparatory school. There they have hung on the dormitory walls for generations. I like to think that a few of these impressionable lads were attracted to Yale by these silent prints that they passed by daily for four years or more. At least a good many of them have spoken to me about the Yale etchings and their early impressions of them.

As the largesse of Yale wore off, the stern realities of being a French householder became more oppressive. The carpenter, the painter, and the heating expert presented reasonable bills, and I was able to pay most of their demands. But the florid character who took care of the masonry and plumbing was outrageous, and I refused to accept his inflated charges. We might have worked the whole matter out in a private conference in the Café du Commerce, but unfortunately this exalted, stubble-chinned, superannuated Romeo decided to elope with a chambermaid from the Chalet de Sylvie in Senlis. On the road to Bordeaux he drove his large Renault into a tree, injuring him and his companion beyond the hope of a romantic *dénouement*. Shortly afterward his wife, who was understandably not amused, sued him for divorce, and sued me for a whopping, catastrophic sum. To defend myself I went through the classic French routine of hiring a *huissier, avocat, avoué,* and *architecte vérificateur,* to protect my interests.

About this time, William Emerson, loyal as ever, entered the family picture, and offered me a post as lecturer in the graphic arts at MIT. My course was to be available to upperclassmen in the School of Architecture and to graduate students interested in the humanities. It was a turning point in the life of the Chamberlains, and we grasped the opportunity with joy. Our dream of living as blissful expatriates in France vanished in the early-morning Senlis mist and the acrimony of French legal manoeuvres.

First we rented our house, fully furnished, to a dashing lieutenant-colonel with intensely piercing pale blue eyes. He was a senior officer with the local regiment of Spahis, and when he came to interview my decisive wife, they were mutually terrified of each other. But a lease of sorts was signed. Then came a hopeful and most naïve conference with my defenders in the litigation with the indignant wife of the wayward plumber. Each stalwart champion of my cause demanded a substantial cash advance, which made serious inroads into our travel budget. Still, we made it. The new Fiat *torpedo* was loaded to the gunwales with suitcases, hat boxes, toys, hampers, cases of prints, and bulging portfolios as we left our house on the rue du Temple and drove cautiously toward Le Havre. Unhappily I had neglected to include a few dozen of my etched copper plates in Rigal's studio, and about six years later they were seized by the Germans and presumably converted into ammunition. A mechanic from Monsieur Terroine's garage took the train to Le Havre and drove "Floyd the Fiat" back to Senlis, and we once again boarded a French ship bound for New York.

This time the change was decisive. We never lived in Senlis again, and we were lucky, in later years, to salvage a part of our furniture and books.

The adventure of moving into the Boston area thrilled all of us except Stephanie, whose only language was French. I made a scouting trip from Greenfield Hill and found a furnished apartment on Middlesex Road in Chestnut Hill. It was popularly known as "The Yellow Peril" and was occupied by charming, neighborly people. Instead of the high stone walls and cobblestones of Senlis, our children reveled in the wide-open spaces, with cement sidewalks for Stephanie and her new tricycle. Little Narcisse was enrolled in the Runkle school, and was furious when they put her back a grade because she had never studied American history. Nobody pulled their shades or closed their shutters at night in the Yellow Peril. There weren't any shutters. On our second day in residence a genial, grey-haired fellow knocked on our door and announced, "Hi, I'm your next-door neighbor. How about coming over tonight for a drink?" In Senlis we had waited

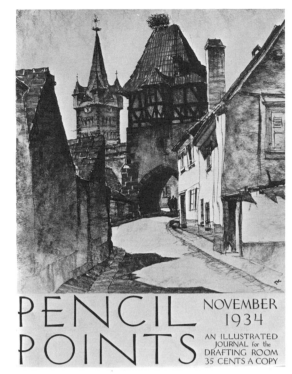

Pencil Points cover, November, 1934

Chateau d'Estaing, study for a
Pencil Points cover

The Donald Moffats

months for our first invitation to tea! Within a fortnight we thoroughly adjusted to this new, fascinating and friendly community. Biscuit has never forgotten her astonishment over the arrival of the "Welcome Wagon." The best thing about the Yellow Peril, however, was the close proximity of our dearest friends, Don and Polly Moffat, who lived about a mile away in Brookline.

Donald Moffat was the son of Frances White Moffat who, as a young widow, married our greatly esteemed William Emerson. An urbane, soft-spoken and most civilized member of the Class of 1916 at Harvard, Don had been one of Professor Copeland's most gifted students. Before our entry into the war, he had also served as a volunteer ambulance driver with the American Field Service, an experience that made him an ardent and permanent francophile. Other things brought us together—an enthusiasm for good wine, gastronomy, and books. He was an imaginative and discriminating master of English prose, and his articles in *The New Yorker* and the *Atlantic* were deft, amusing, and remarkably observant. He published two gay and affectionate books concerning the adventures of American families living in France, as well as a volume of essays on more serious themes entitled *The Prejudices of Mr. Pennyfeather*.

His pretty and animated wife, Polly, was the youngest of three daughters of the painter Joseph De Camp, and grew up in the atmosphere of a portraitist's studio. Her father painted scores of celebrities in his day, including the best-known portrait of Theodore Roosevelt, and he was commissioned to paint the signing of the Treaty of Versailles. Unfortunately none of the key participants consented to sit for a definitive portrait, and Joseph De Camp's heroic painting of the ceremony in the Hall of Mirrors never got beyond the skillfully conceived preliminary oil sketch, painted on the spot.

Donald Moffat's perceptive and sophisticated prose was the perfect complement to my pictures. Aided by his thoughtful and witty text, pictures assumed a new significance. In all, we produced five books together, and in each Don's words gave the illustrations an added meaning.

Later, when I embarked on lengthy manuscripts of my own, Don always offered to go over them and weed out the inconsistencies. He was a superb copy editor. He threw out my flamboyant adjectives without mercy, and made me distrust the vague word "colorful" which I've rarely dared use again. To this exacting, charming and loyal friend, I owe a debt of infinite gratitude. The Moffat daughters are close companions of our own girls, carrying this affection to a new generation.

As we settled down in Chestnut Hill, I bought a large, black, second-hand automobile that had obviously belonged to a gangster-undertaker, and for the first time we had a radio to indoctrinate our little girls into the splendors of Donald Duck, cavity-free toothpaste and cereals that went snap, crackle and pop.

The forum for my lectures in the graphic arts was a large abandoned basement room in the Rogers Building that had once been a chemistry lab. It needed a bit of fixing, but the janitorial staff were most helpful.

I—Needling the copper plate

II—Inking the steel-faced plate with a rubber roller

III—Hand wiping the plate

IV—Laying moistened paper on the inked plate

V—Plate and paper going through the old French press

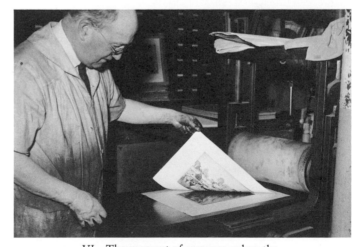

VI—The moment of suspense, when the fresh impression is peeled from the plate

Six steps in the making of a drypoint
demonstrated by the author

Espalion

Apse of St. John the Divine,
New York

A double semicircle of wide-armed student chairs was achieved, and nonglaring overhead lights did much to dispel the ghostly atmosphere of the place. With extraordinary good luck I came upon a fine old French etching press, and a functioning lithographic press as well. With the addition of a blackboard and stands for tacking up prints, I was in business. My one-hour lectures took place twice a week, and were attended by mature, thoughtful and acquisitive students who were a joy to a neophyte teacher. They seemed to enjoy the curriculum, as well they might, for I did all the work. Most courses at MIT aren't on any such basis. During the term I demonstrated various sketching techniques—graphite and carbon pencil, pen-and-ink, dry-brush ink drawings, square Conté crayon and wash drawings. These were followed by demonstrations of the copperplate medium. I tried to repeat the basic teaching that Monsieur Edouard Léon had imparted so well, with a smattering of the Royal College of Art added. In succeeding weeks I made demonstration plates in etching, drypoint, engraving and aquatint, and pulled a few impressions of each plate. The students drew lots for them, and this made a real hit. Two lectures on lithography ended the term.

The boys responded well, and before my teaching days were over, two eminent members of the faculty, Professor Seaver, the art historian, and Dean Bunker of the Graduate School, joined the class and became adept amateur etchers. The only required homework for the students consisted of visits to the print collections in the Museum of Fine Arts in Boston. Successively they went through collections of the old masters, Dürer, Rembrandt and their followers, then the English masters of etching and mezzotint and the fine French portraitists, and finally such modern masters as Lepère, Legros, Meryon, Zorn, Whistler, Bone, Cameron and McBey. The boys seemed to enjoy it as a change from their technical studies, and wrote such good papers that I couldn't bear to give any of them a grade less than B. This was an *imprudence fatale,* for word soon got around that mine was a "lunch course," and in succeeding years I had a miscellany of charming and ingenious students who needed a good mark but weren't too keen to work for it.

Most of the graduate students were total strangers to Boston when they arrived for the fall term, and without authorization from anybody, I devoted a few minutes of the first lecture to gastronomy. How to find a good meal at a low price was something that interested every student, and without hesitation I sent them to Durgin-Park's Market Dining Room opposite Quincy market. At that time the restaurant offered a copious beef stew for exactly twenty-five cents, accompanied by generous slices of tea cake and butter at no extra charge. It was the epicurean bargain of Boston, and the out-of-town students came back glowing with satisfaction.

The Great Court,
MIT in Cambridge

After a few years in the Rogers Building, the whole School of Architecture was moved to new quarters in Cambridge, and my studio lost all of its antique charm. In a clean classroom lighted by an immense window the lectures on the graphic arts continued. By this time the schedule had been changed, and I gave but one weekly lecture, from eleven to one P.M. on Saturday, the last gasp of the week. Most of the lads were attentive to my perspiring efforts, but I had inherited a few gay blades among the student body who obviously spent their Friday nights in varied Bacchanalia. By now this must be an extinct species, considering MIT's heavy work load, but a few playboys survived at that time. They made my lecture as a rule, but then dozed gently through most of it. One sheepish fellow never did hear me beyond the first five minutes, and I was obliged to give him an F, the only one of my teaching career. The more serious students showed great interest, however, and many of them made their first etchings, drypoints and lithographs in the new studio. I have a small collection of them still, and they demonstrate once again the short step between architecture and the graphic arts.

Among these students were many destined for future fame. Gordon Bunshaft, the gifted designer and partner of Skidmore, Owings and Merrill, was an attentive listener. So was I. M. Pei, the extraordinary Chinese-American designer, who is today one of America's greatest architects. Harry Weese, a superb draftsman, made a few skillful plates in the studio, and went on to be famous in the Middle West for his imaginative architecture. Another serious student was Francis Sargent, at present the lieutenant-governor of Massachusetts. The list could go on for a paragraph or more. Several members of the graphic arts class became print collectors, but as far as I know, none of them took up etching as a profession. The course prospered for several years in the thirties, but finally dissolved with the advent of World War II.

87

Acorn Street, Boston,
an "American Scene" postcard

Washington Square, New York,
an "American Scene" postcard

During frequent visits to Yale I had often spoken to George Parmly Day about my most persistent complaint—the lack of good postcards in America. Whereas the traveler could find fine photographic cards in Britain and on the Continent, the choice offered him in the United States was particularly poor—usually cheap, garish, colored cards in total bad taste. As an example of what might be done at home, I showed him some rich sepia gravure cards published by Yvon in France. He must have been impressed, for months later he wrote and asked me to come to New Haven to discuss good photographic postcards of Connecticut. The state was about to celebrate its tercentenary in 1935, and the Yale University Press was interested in publishing a series of postcard views to commemorate the event. Mr. Day asked me to undertake the project. The shift from an expensive portfolio of etchings to a five-cent postcard was rather abrupt, but I had really asked for it, and accepted the offer with enthusiasm.

The first step was to buy a good view camera, a Carl Zeiss product called an Orix. It had a beautiful sharp *Tessar* 1:4.5 lens and a rising front, and used 10 x 15 cm. film packs. With a tripod, a black cloth to improve visibility on the ground glass, and a French beret, I set out on a planned itinerary of Connecticut in a small car, and followed country roads that crisscrossed the state. It was an idyllic undertaking as long as the weather was good. The camera seemed refreshingly rapid compared to the painstaking time necessary for a drawing. This was my first commercial venture in photography. The Tercentenary postcards appeared on schedule in 1935 and consisted of four sets of thirty cards each, devoted to Early Meeting Houses, Historic Houses, Doorways, Taverns, and Public Buildings, and the Connecticut countryside. The sets were printed in sheet-fed gravure by the Photogravure and Color Company in New York, and possessed a velvety richness comparable to the French cards. Everyone seemed pleased, and we lost no time in adopting "The American Scene" as our trademark. Sixty postcard views of Yale came next, and the reception they received encouraged us to branch out into New England. Within two years new sets were issued on Boston, Historic Plymouth, Historic Concord, Lexington and Cambridge, and Cape Cod. Finally I spent many lonely summer Sundays photographing the splendors of New York City for a last set of sixty views.

Artistically the cards were more than acceptable, but as time rolled on it became clear that they were not a commercial success. There weren't enough postcard buyers who cared about quality, and besides, the postcard business was on a cut-throat competitive basis that made our venture seem naïve and ineffective. The Yale cards were reprinted occasionally, but the other subjects were allowed to sell out and rest in peace. "The American Scene" vanished gracefully, and this is just as well, since color was on its way, destined to supersede the black-and-white card completely. Still, this was a moment to record with gratitude, for it was the beginning of a long series of camera expeditions that later blossomed into book form.

Suburban Chestnut Hill was fine, but all of us longed for a country town near Boston as the second year of teaching approached. We

Old Marblehead from Crocker Park

shopped about in the black gangster car for a new location. A leak had developed in the windshield of the car, and a fine fungus growth developed, to the delight of the children. We refused to molest our lichen, which finally achieved the dimensions of a small, projecting pumpkin pie. We explored desirable towns in the environs—Concord, Wellesley, Hingham, and finally, Marblehead, where I had sometimes gone on sketching expeditions while a student. We weren't a maritime family, in spite of so many Atlantic crossings, but there was something about this old pre-Revolutionary seaport that attracted us. It wasn't an active fishing port like Gloucester, or an arty one such as Rockport. But it was filled with ruddy, clean-cut yachtsmen and attractive "summer people." The main shopping section of Marblehead was deplorable—a succession of cinder-block cubicles—but it was isolated from the old part of the town, which contained fine elm-shaded streets and many dignified eighteenth-century mansions.

Once again William Emerson stepped into the picture. He sent us to his friend I. Howland Jones, a Boston architect who lived in Marblehead and who found us a furnished house next to his, on Tucker

Fisherman's Shanty, Marblehead

Summer Street, Marblehead

Saunderstown Fields

Street. It was large and comfortable with a view of the harbor, and one room could be adapted as a studio. I set up my white tracing paper screen and began to make drypoints of a few favorite French sketches. Stephanie was enrolled in Tower School, and we became members of a car pool that transported shouting, squirming urchins back and forth to their classes. Here the comparison with France was not favorable, and we thought often of our demure daughter, holding the maid's hand and stepping daintily along the cobblestones on her way to school in Senlis. In Marblehead, life was more robust. Softball and scrimmage were the accepted games on the grassy common adjoining the town hall. As for the older set, we were invited to join the badminton club, which fortunately was not totally dedicated to swatting that silly bird. More convivial rewards followed the last play-off, and we decided that this seaport town, like Chestnut Hill, harbored any number of charming people.

This was an active winter for drypoints, and I had a variety of promising drawings to put onto copper. One was a busy and quite majestic view of Quimper, in Brittany. The huge mass of the cathedral rose up at the end of a street of towering timbered houses. Another was Burgundian, a view of the château village of Le Rochepot surrounded by vineyards and entitled "Burgundy Village." A third was "Essex

Normandy Doorway

91

Quimper

Stonington Sunset

Village," a view of the somnolent English hamlet of Newport. There were American subjects too, including a sylvan view of Marblehead, our new home. It showed Summer Street in full foliage, and won the John Taylor Arms Prize when exhibited at the Society of American Etchers in New York. "Stonington Sunset" was a rather bold interpretation of a Yankee fishing port, and "Saunderstown Fields" was a serene Rhode Island landscape.

Deprived of my faithful French printer, I had to print the early states and the final editions of all these plates myself. The etching press at MIT saw a great deal of service, and I developed slightly bulging biceps during those months. By using the wonderfully receptive Shogun paper, made in Japan, I was usually able to capture the delicacy of fine drypoint lines as well as the subtlety of veiled tones of etching ink. The prints stood up well against their predecessors, but I don't recommend plate printing as a profession. It's too exhausting.

The Village Square, Besse-en-Chandesse

Photography began to take up much of my time, but in 1938 I finished three drypoints of interest. One of these was a horizontal view of Chestnut Street in neighboring Salem. Many critics consider it to be the finest street in America. "Springtime in Salem" shows a few of the three-story mansions built by sea captains and merchant princes in the early nineteenth century, framed in light spring foliage.

93

Springtime in Salem

In 1940 it was accepted at the exhibition of American etchings at the New York World's Fair, where the jury of awards ignored it completely. But the public was also allowed to vote for a favorite print, and when the ballots were counted late in the year, this Salem drypoint received the most votes. I'm not sure what moral should be drawn from this, if any.

Sentimental attachment to the old Rogers Building in Boston led me to make a drypoint of this notable landmark before it was torn down to make way for an insurance building. Finally, the prim little Christ Church in Cambridge, where George and Martha Washington worshipped on New Year's Eve, 1775, proved a tempting etching subject, and I tried hard to catch its simple wooden tower bathed in springtime sunlight. This proved to be a popular print, especially as a wedding present for young couples who were married in the church. The sales graph always went up in June.

Along with so much printmaking, I spent most of my spare time on a totally different project—a wine chart. My interest in the red and white wines of France has always been intense and relentless, and I was determined to combine the graphic arts with gastronomy in one package that would appeal to all gastronomes and oenophiles. A richly decorative chart, brightened with maps, vignettes and pen-and-

94

Christ Church, Cambridge

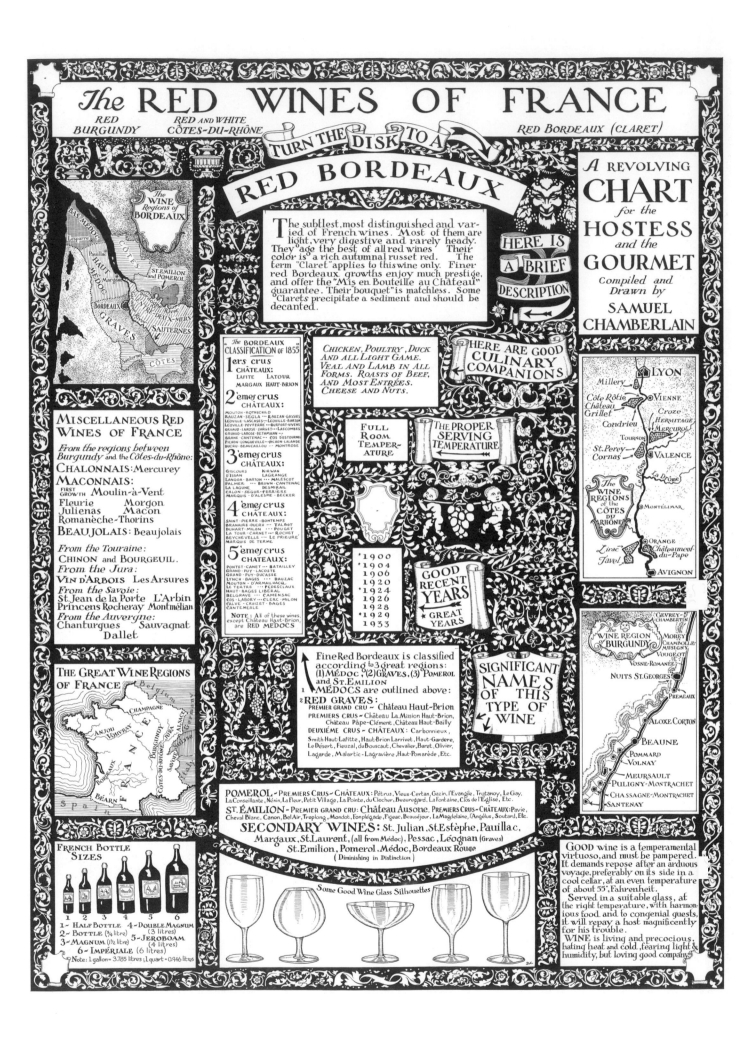

The RED WINES OF FRANCE

RED BURGUNDY — RED AND WHITE CÔTES-DU-RHÔNE — RED BORDEAUX (CLARET)

TURN THE DISK TO A

RED BORDEAUX

HERE IS A BRIEF DESCRIPTION

A REVOLVING CHART for the HOSTESS and the GOURMET

Compiled and Drawn by SAMUEL CHAMBERLAIN

The WINE Regions of BORDEAUX

The subtlest, most distinguished and varied of French wines. Most of them are light, very digestive and rarely heady. They age the best of all red wines. Their color is a rich autumnal russet red. The term "Claret" applies to this wine only. Finer red Bordeaux growths enjoy much prestige, and offer the "Mis en Bouteille au Château" guarantee. Their bouquet is matchless. Some Clarets precipitate a sediment and should be decanted.

MISCELLANEOUS RED WINES OF FRANCE

From the regions between Burgundy and the Côtes-du-Rhône:

CHALONNAIS: Mercurey

MACONNAIS:
FIRST GROWTH Moulin-à-Vent
Fleurie   Morgon
Julienas   Macon
Romanèche-Thorins

BEAUJOLAIS: Beaujolais

From the Touraine:
CHINON and BOURGEUIL

From the Jura:
VIN D'ARBOIS Les Arsures

From the Savoie:
St. Jean de la Porte L'Arbin
Princens Rocheray Montmélian

From the Auvergne:
Chanturgues   Sauvagnat
Dallet

THE GREAT WINE REGIONS OF FRANCE

The BORDEAUX CLASSIFICATION of 1855

1ers crus CHÂTEAUX:
LAFITE   LATOUR
MARGAUX HAUT-BRION

2èmes crus CHÂTEAUX:
MOUTON-ROTHSCHILD
RAUZAN-SEGLA ··· RAUZAN-GASSIES
LEOVILLE-LASCASES ··· LEOVILLE-BARTON
LEOVILLE-POYFERRÉ ··· DURFORT-VIVENS
GRUAUD-LAROSE-SARGET ··· LASCOMBES
GRUAUD-LAROSE-BETHMANN ···
BRANE-CANTENAC ··· COS DESTOURNEL
PICHON-LONGUEVILLE ··· PICHON-LALANDE
DUCRU-BEAUCAILLOU ··· MONTROSE

3èmes crus CHÂTEAUX:
GISCOURS   KIRWAN
D'ISSAN   LAGRANGE
LANGOA-BARTON ··· MALESCOT
PALMER ···   BROWN-CANTENAC
LA LAGUNE   DESMIRAIL
CALON-SEGUR-FERRIERE
MARQUIS-D'ALESME-BECKER

4èmes crus CHÂTEAUX:
SAINT-PIERRE-BONTEMPS
BRANAIRE-DUCRU ··· TALBOT
DUHART-MILON ··· POUGET
LA TOUR-CARNET ··· ROCHET
BEYCHEVELLE ··· LE PRIEURÉ
MARQUIS DE TERME

5èmes crus CHÂTEAUX:
PONTET-CANET ··· BATAILLEY
GRAND-PUY-LACOSTE
GRAND-PUY-DUCASSE
LYNCH-BAGES ··· DAUZAC
MOUTON-D'ARMAILHACQ···
LE TERTRE ··· PÉDESCLAUX
HAUT-BAGES LIBERAL
BELGRAVE ··· CAMENSAC
COS-LABORY ··· CLERC-MILON
CALVE-CROIZET-BAGES
CANTEMERLE

NOTE: All of these wines, except Château Haut-Brion, are RED MEDOCS

CHICKEN, POULTRY, DUCK AND ALL LIGHT GAME. VEAL AND LAMB IN ALL FORMS. ROASTS OF BEEF, AND MOST ENTRÉES. CHEESE AND NUTS.

HERE ARE GOOD CULINARY COMPANIONS

FULL ROOM TEMPERATURE

THE PROPER SERVING TEMPERATURE

*1900
*1904
1906
1920
*1924
1926
1928
*1929
1933

GOOD RECENT YEARS

★ GREAT YEARS

The WINE REGIONS of the CÔTES DU RHÔNE

LYON
Millery
Côte Rôtie
Château Grillet
Condrieu
St. Perey
Cornas
VIENNE
Croze
HERMITAGE
MERCUROL
Tournon
VALENCE
La Drôme
MONTÉLIMAR
Lirac
Javel
ORANGE
Châteauneuf-du-Pape
AVIGNON

Fine Red Bordeaux is classified according to 3 great regions: (1) MÉDOC (2) GRAVES, (3) POMEROL and St. EMILION

1 MÉDOCS are outlined above:

2 RED GRAVES:
PREMIER GRAND CRU ~ Château Haut-Brion
PREMIERS CRUS ~ Château La Mission Haut-Brion, Château Pâpe-Clément, Château Haut-Bailly
DEUXIÈME CRUS ~ CHÂTEAUX: Carbonnieux, Smith Haut-Lafitte, Haut-Brion Larrivet, Haut-Gardère, Le Désert, Fieuzal, duBouscaut, Chevalier, Baret, Olivier, Lagarde, Malartic-Lagravière, Haut-Pomarède, Etc.

SIGNIFICANT NAMES OF THIS TYPE OF WINE

The WINE REGION of BURGUNDY

GEVREY-CHAMBERTIN
MOREY
CHAMBOLLE-MUSIGNY
VOUGEOT
VOSNE-ROMANÉE
NUITS ST. GEORGES
PREMEAUX
ALOXE CORTON
BEAUNE
POMMARD
VOLNAY
MEURSAULT
PULIGNY-MONTRACHET
CHASSAGNE-MONTRACHET
SANTENAY

POMEROL ~ PREMIERS CRUS ~ CHÂTEAUX: Pétrus, Vieux-Certan, Gazin, l'Evangile, Trotanoy, Le Gay, La Conseillante, Nénin, La Fleur, Petit Village, La Pointe, du Clocher, Beauregard, La Fontaine, Clos de l'Eglise, Etc.

St. ÉMILION ~ PREMIER GRAND CRU ~ Château Ausone. PREMIERS CRUS ~ CHÂTEAUX: Pavie, Cheval Blanc, Canon, Bel Air, Troplong, Mondot, Fonplégade, Figeac, Beauséjour, La Magdelaine, l'Angélus, Soutard, Etc.

SECONDARY WINES: St. Julian, St. Estèphe, Pauillac, Margaux, St. Laurent, (all from Médoc), Pessac, Léognan (Graves) St. Emilion, Pomerol, Médoc, Bordeaux Rouge
(Diminishing in Distinction)

FRENCH BOTTLE SIZES

1 ~ HALF BOTTLE   4 ~ DOUBLE MAGNUM (3 litres)
2 ~ BOTTLE (⅞ litre)   5 ~ JEROBOAM (4 litres)
3 ~ MAGNUM (1½ litre)   6 ~ IMPÉRIALE (6 litres)
Note: 1 gallon = 3.785 litres; 1 quart = 0.946 litres

Some Good Wine Glass Silhouettes

GOOD wine is a temperamental virtuoso, and must be pampered. It demands repose after an arduous voyage, preferably on its side in a cool cellar, at an even temperature of about 55° Fahrenheit.

Served in a suitable glass, at the right temperature, with harmonious food and to congenial guests, it will repay a host magnificently for his trouble.

WINE is living and precocious, hating heat and cold, fearing light & humidity, but loving good company.

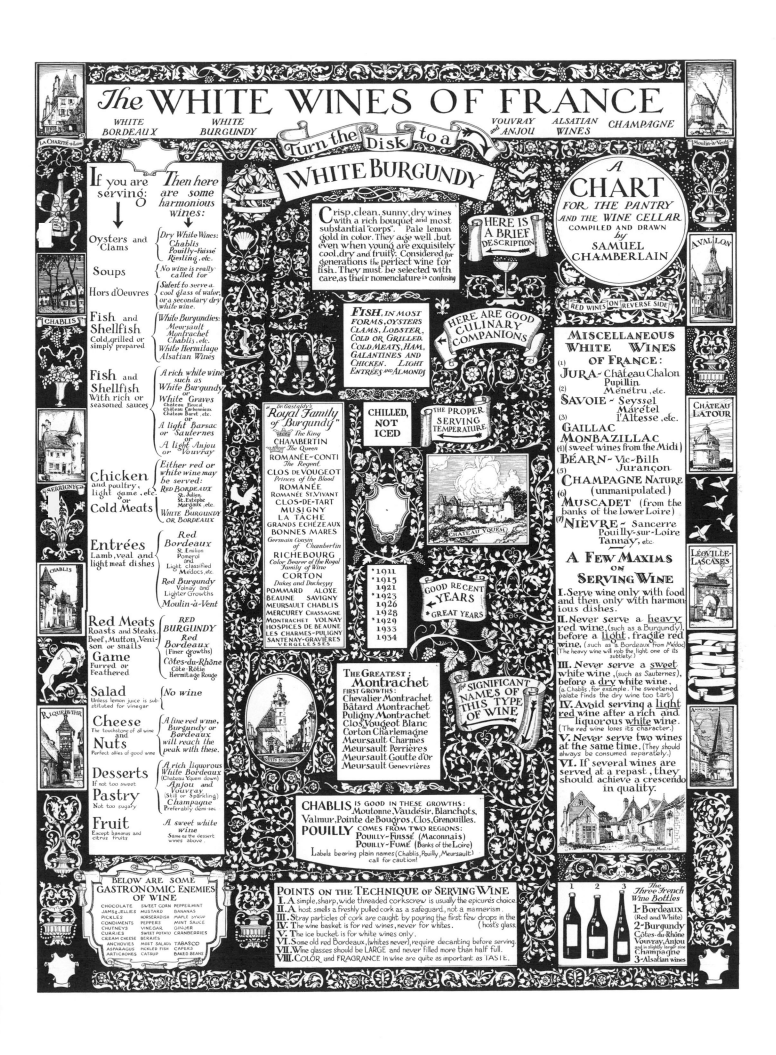

The WHITE WINES OF FRANCE

WHITE BORDEAUX · WHITE BURGUNDY · VOUVRAY and ANJOU · ALSATIAN WINES · CHAMPAGNE

Turn the Disk to a

WHITE BURGUNDY

A CHART FOR THE PANTRY AND THE WINE CELLAR COMPILED AND DRAWN by SAMUEL CHAMBERLAIN

HERE IS A BRIEF DESCRIPTION

RED WINES ON REVERSE SIDE

Crisp, clean, sunny, dry wines with a rich bouquet and most substantial "corps". Pale lemon gold in color. They age well, but even when young are exquisitely cool, dry and fruity. Considered for generations the perfect wine for fish. They must be selected with care, as their nomenclature is confusing

If you are serving:

Oysters and Clams	Dry White Wines: Chablis, Pouilly-Fuissé, Riesling, etc.
Soups	No wine is really called for
Hors d'Oeuvres	Safest to serve a cool glass of water, or a secondary dry white wine.
Fish and Shellfish — Cold, grilled or simply prepared	White Burgundies: Meursault, Montrachet, Chablis, etc. White Hermitage, Alsatian Wines
Fish and Shellfish — With rich or seasoned sauces	A rich white wine such as White Burgundy or White Graves — Château Fieuzal, Château Carbonnieux, Château Baret, etc. — or A light Barsac or Sauternes or A light Anjou or Vouvray
Chicken and poultry, light game, etc. or Cold Meats	Either red or white wine may be served: Red Bordeaux — St. Julien, St. Estèphe, Margaux, etc. White Burgundy or Bordeaux
Entrées — Lamb, veal and light meat dishes	Red Bordeaux — St. Emilion, Pomerol and Light classified Médocs, etc. Red Burgundy — Volnay and Lighter Growths — Moulin-à-Vent
Red Meats — Roasts and Steaks, Beef, Mutton, Venison or snails	RED BURGUNDY Red Bordeaux (Finer growths) Côtes-du-Rhône, Côte-Rôtie, Hermitage Rouge
Game — Furred or Feathered	
Salad — Unless lemon juice is substituted for vinegar	No wine
Cheese — The touchstone of all wine and Nuts — Perfect allies of good wine	A fine red wine, Burgundy or Bordeaux will reach the peak with these.
Desserts — If not too sweet, Pastry — Not too sugary	A rich liquorous White Bordeaux (Château Yquem down) Anjou and Vouvray (Still or Sparkling) Champagne Preferably demi-sec
Fruit — Except bananas and citrus fruits	A sweet white wine — Same as the dessert wines above.

Here are some harmonious wines:

HERE ARE GOOD CULINARY COMPANIONS

FISH, IN MOST FORMS, OYSTERS, CLAMS, LOBSTER, COLD OR GRILLED. COLD MEATS, HAM, GALANTINES AND CHICKEN. LIGHT ENTRÉES AND ALMONDS

"Dr. Gastaldy's Royal Family of Burgundy"

The King — CHAMBERTIN
The Queen — ROMANÉE-CONTI
The Regent — CLOS DE VOUGEOT
Princes of the Blood — ROMANÉE, Romanée St. Vivant, CLOS-DE-TART, MUSIGNY, LA TÂCHE, GRANDS ECHÉZEAUX, BONNES MARES
Germain Cousin of Chambertin — RICHEBOURG
Color Bearer of the Royal Family of Wine — CORTON
Dukes and Duchesses — POMMARD, ALOXE, BEAUNE, SAVIGNY, MEURSAULT, CHABLIS, MERCUREY, CHASSAGNE, MONTRACHET, VOLNAY, HOSPICES DE BEAUNE, LES CHARMES-PULIGNY, SANTENAY-GRAVIÈRES, VERGELESSES

CHILLED, NOT ICED

THE PROPER SERVING TEMPERATURE

CHÂTEAU YQUEM

GOOD RECENT YEARS · *GREAT YEARS

*1911
*1915
1921
*1923
1926
1928
*1929
1933
1934

THE GREATEST: Montrachet

FIRST GROWTHS:
Chevalier Montrachet
Bâtard Montrachet
Puligny Montrachet
Clos Vougeot Blanc
Corton Charlemagne
Meursault Charmes
Meursault Perrières
Meursault Goutte d'Or
Meursault Genevrières

THE SIGNIFICANT NAMES OF THIS TYPE OF WINE

CHABLIS IS GOOD IN THESE GROWTHS: Moutonne, Vaudésir, Blanchots, Valmur, Pointe de Bougros, Clos, Grenouilles,

POUILLY COMES FROM TWO REGIONS:
Pouilly-Fuissé (Maconnais)
Pouilly-Fumé (Banks of the Loire)
Labels bearing plain names (Chablis, Pouilly, Meursault) call for caution!

MISCELLANEOUS WHITE WINES OF FRANCE:

(1) JURA ~ Château Chalon, Pupillin, Ménétru, etc.
(2) SAVOIE ~ Seyssel, Marétel, l'Altesse, etc.
(3) GAILLAC, MONBAZILLAC
(4) (sweet wines from the Midi) BÉARN ~ Vic-Bilh, Jurançon
(5) CHAMPAGNE NATURE (unmanipulated)
(6) MUSCADET (from the banks of the lower Loire)
(7) NIÈVRE ~ Sancerre, Pouilly-sur-Loire, Tannay, etc.

A FEW MAXIMS ON SERVING WINE

I. Serve wine only with food and then only with harmonious dishes.
II. Never serve a heavy red wine, (such as a Burgundy), before a light, fragile red wine, (such as a Bordeaux from Médoc) (The heavy wine will rob the light one of its subtlety.)
III. Never serve a sweet white wine, (such as Sauternes), before a dry white wine, (a Chablis, for example. The sweetened palate finds the dry wine too tart.)
IV. Avoid serving a light red wine after a rich and liquorous white wine. (The red wine loses its character.)
V. Never serve two wines at the same time. (They should always be consumed separately.)
VI. If several wines are served at a repast, they should achieve a crescendo in quality.

Puligny-Montrachet

BELOW ARE SOME GASTRONOMIC ENEMIES OF WINE

CHOCOLATE	SWEET CORN	PEPPERMINT
JAMS & JELLIES	MUSTARD	BANANAS
PICKLES	HORSERADISH	MAPLE SYRUP
CONDIMENTS	PEPPERS	MINT SAUCE
CHUTNEYS	VINEGAR	GINGER
CURRIES	SWEET POTATO	CRANBERRIES
CREAM CHEESE	BERRIES	
ANCHOVIES	MOST SALADS	TABASCO
ASPARAGUS	PICKLED FISH	CAPERS
ARTICHOKES	CATSUP	BAKED BEANS

POINTS ON THE TECHNIQUE of SERVING WINE

I. A simple, sharp, wide threaded corkscrew is usually the epicure's choice.
II. A host smells a freshly pulled cork as a safeguard, not a mannerism.
III. Stray particles of cork are caught by pouring the first few drops in the host's glass.
IV. The wine basket is for red wines, never for whites.
V. The ice bucket is for white wines only.
VI. Some old red Bordeaux, (whites never), require decanting before serving.
VII. Wine glasses should be LARGE and never filled more than half full.
VIII. COLOR and FRAGRANCE in wine are quite as important as TASTE.

The Three French Wine Bottles

1- Bordeaux (Red and White)
2- Burgundy Côtes-du-Rhône, Vouvray, Anjou and in slightly larger size Champagne
3- Alsatian wines

LA CHARITÉ-s-Loire · CHABLIS · SERRIGNY · CHABLIS · RIQUEWIHR · Moulin-à-Vent · AVALLON · CHÂTEAU LATOUR · LÉOVILLE-LASCASES · AMMERSCHWIHR · NUITS ST GEORGES

Harlow House, 1677, Plymouth, Massachusetts,
from *A Small House in the Sun*

Parson Capen House, 1683, Topsfield, Massachusetts,
from *A Small House in the Sun*

ink sketches, was the result. Everything was hand-lettered. Openings of various sizes were cut in the chart, and these revealed information on various wines, lettered on a disk. Turn the disk to the right place and all the pertinent data on red Bordeaux, red Burgundy, or Côtes-du-Rhône wines would be progressively revealed. There was a descriptive essay on each wine, mention of good culinary companions, proper serving temperature, good recent years, and the significant names of each type of wine. On the other side of the disk was assembled the same information on the great French white wines, those of Burgundy, Bordeaux, Champagne, Vouvray and Anjou, and Alsace. On the two faces of the chart were drawings of typical bottles and wine glasses, and suggestions of what harmonious wine to serve with food, from oysters, soups, fish, shellfish, chicken, red meats, game and cheese, down to desserts and pastry. There were pointers on the technique of serving wine and on secondary vintages, and a list of gastronomic enemies of wine, from anchovies to Tabasco sauce.

I am absolutely appalled at the magnitude of this undertaking, and feel now that my days would have been spent far more usefully in reading Dr. Eliot's five-foot bookshelf. Once the chart was finished, I showed it to several publishers, all of whom turned it down because it presented too many production problems. It has been in my portfolio all these years, a reminder of a magnificent and earnest way to waste one's time.

Springtime of 1936 arrived in a burst of glory, and the combination of a car, a camera, and a chronic wanderlust had resulted in an irrepressible urge to travel. With the family well entrenched in Marblehead, I began to explore the other five New England states, hoping some day to know them as well as I knew Connecticut. It turned out to be a beautiful spring and summer, blessed by bountiful sunshine. With film packs stacked high in the trunk of the car, I wandered from Cape Cod to the Berkshires, followed the eccentric coastline from Point Judith to West Quoddy Head, Maine, and then strayed through New Hampshire and Vermont. All sorts of photogenic subjects appeared along the way—seascapes, covered bridges, country churches, farmhouses and stately mansions.

I was attracted to old houses, particularly the small ones that could provide ideas for contemporary housebuilders. Good examples of the old pitch-roofed cottage, the gambrel-roofed house and the small two-story dwelling are scattered all over New England, and at the end of the summer's travels I had accumulated a respectable collection of sharp, sunny photographs of historic small houses. Here was promising material for a book, and I made up a careful dummy, complete with pasted pictures and captions, of a ninety-six-page book hopefully entitled *A Small House in the Sun*.

The dummy was mailed to Paul Wenzel, head of the Architectural Book Publishing Company in New York. He had been kind to my earlier efforts, and I rather thought this would intrigue him. Later when I paid him a visit in his office on 46th Street he broke the news gently that this New England subject was too far removed from his field, and suggested that I show the dummy to some other publisher. I put the dummy in its Manila envelope, shook hands, and was about to leave when Mr. Wenzel's grandson suddenly appeared from the depths of the stockroom. He apparently didn't want me to disappear, and suggested that we have lunch together. His name was Walter Frese, and something obviously was weighing on his mind. Around the corner on 47th Street was a Mexican restaurant where a fine murder had occurred only the previous week. We found a booth, and over enchiladas and chili, crackers and beer, Mr. Frese unburdened himself. He was acutely distressed to see this book rejected by his grandfather. Furthermore, he had long harbored the desire to become a publisher himself. Would I give him permission to publish this book on New England houses? Over guava jelly, cream cheese and another beer we came to an agreement, and Walter had the dummy under his arm as we left the Alamo Restaurant.

A Small House in the Sun was published in 1936. It was printed in sheet-fed gravure, and the pages measured 12¼ by 9¼ inches. This was the maiden publication of Hastings House Publishers, Inc., now in its thirtieth year. In those three decades Walter and I have produced almost fifty books together, and today have others in the planning stage. Hastings House has earned an enviable reputation in the field of non-fiction, and has victoriously weathered the storms that assail all smaller publishers.

Nearly all of the books that Walter Frese and I have produced together have been printed in sheet-fed gravure. It is a process that lends depth, warmth, and richness to photographs and drawings. In contrast to half-tone, which, under magnification, is revealed as a series of round dots, gravure is a fabric of closely woven hash marks that record extreme detail and rich contrasts at the same time. Pages of positive photographic films are transferred to large sheets of sensitized copper under strong arc lights. The copper is then etched with acid. A great deal of "make ready" is necessary before the printing run finally gets under way, but the results are lustrous, with strong contrast.

During the preparation of this first book, I visited the Photogravure and Color Company in New York where a violently cross-eyed Swede named Olaf explained the whole process. After this visit it became clear that much better results could be obtained in sheet-fed gravure by submitting negatives for reproduction, rather than black-and-white glossy prints. Using negatives meant one less photographic step, namely rephotographing the glossy print. It also meant that a certain amount of manipulating—dodging here and holding back there— could be used by the photographer while projecting the negative on the positive film. The same company, now moved to New Jersey, still prints most of our illustrated books and calendars.

This first photographic book was hardly a sensation at its initial appearance, but it was the first olive out of the publishing bottle, and many more were to follow. Cape Cod was an irresistible subject, and I spent months photographing this fascinating hook of land all the way from the Sagamore bridge to the last glimpse of Provincetown sand. Commercialism had not greatly scarred the Cape at that time, and *Cape Cod in the Sun* is filled with views of pristine freshness. It ap-

The Village Street, Yarmouthport,
from *Cape Cod in the Sun*

The Dunes at Eastham,
from *Cape Cod in the Sun*

Cottage at East Sandwich,
from *Cape Cod in the Sun*

The "McBey picture," Falmouth Harbor, from *Cape Cod in the Sun*

Fireplace in the Abraham Browne, Jr.,
House (1663), Watertown, Massachusetts,
from *Beyond New England Thresholds*

peared in 1937, and revealed the bow-roofed shingled cottages, the turned white fence posts, shingled windmills, lighthouses, dunes, inlets and luxuriant pink roses that are the hallmark of the Cape.

One extraordinary coincidence turned up in connection with this book. On page 27 I wrote a caption for a view of Falmouth Harbor and added "One wishes that a James McBey or a Seymour Haden were on hand to record the placidity of this scene, an etcher's subject if there ever was one." A few years later, to my astonishment, a letter came from James McBey, the famed Scottish etcher. He had been staying with friends on Cape Cod, and had made numerous sketching expeditions. On returning to his host's library he thumbed through a copy of *Cape Cod in the Sun,* read my caption and to his stupefaction found that he had made a sketch on precisely the spot I had pictured. This led to more correspondence, I assure you, and I finally lured McBey and his attractive young American wife to my studio in Marblehead. They were hurriedly on their way somewhere else, however, and instead of the sumptuous French luncheon at home that I had planned, we repaired to the local diner where I mournfully watched the great McBey consume a hamburger.

One of the subjects that interests our readers most is antiquity, specifically early American antiques and interiors. This was the theme of my next large gravure book, *Beyond New England Thresholds,* published in 1937. It illustrates many interiors, from the sparse early seventeenth-century houses such as the Parson Capen House in Topsfield, to the splendor of Samuel McIntire's work in Salem and the opulence of Gore Place in Waltham, perhaps New England's most imposing mansion. All of these interior views were made with time exposures on my faithful Orix view camera. This was before I began to rely on floodlights, and all of the interiors were taken with natural daylight only. This book has proven to be a hardy perennial, and a new printing has recently been distributed in 1967, its thirtieth birthday.

During these months of travel on the side roads of New England, I learned many of the vicissitudes of being a cameraman. The architectural photographer does not have to face the knockdown-and-dragout battles of the cameramen who cover the news, but he finds himself on the same lowly social scale. Try invading the campus of a college or a preparatory school with a camera, tripod, and black cloth, and you will see what I mean. You might as well be an organ grinder with a monkey. Schoolchildren are not quite as scornful as college boys. How many hundreds, nay thousands of times, have I seen a grimacing youngster stride toward me shouting "Hey, Mistah, take my pitcha!" The children in Britain, France and Italy don't take such a bold approach. They believe that if they asked me to take their picture, I might accept, and send their father the bill. So the English lad warns "Watch the birdie," and the French *gamin* says "*Regard le petit oiseau*" while the Italian lad murmurs something about the *piccolo uccello*. No litigation is in sight.

My camera has never been smashed by an irate and unwilling subject, but occasionally there have been tiffs with resentful houseowners. In most cases I defer to their wishes, and turn my lens in other directions. Occasionally I stand up to my rights, however, and photograph whatever is visible from the public highway, as is my right. One of my photographs shows an irate man shaking his fist at me from the front porch, while his wife madly waves her apron from the garden. They were out to ruin my picture, and they did. In another Connecticut town I encountered a farmer who took a violent dislike to my low canary-colored sports car, and particularly to my French beret. "What kind of hat is that?" he shouted, followed by a few phrases that I will omit. "If you don't get out of here, I'll send my dog after you!" he bellowed. I hesitated, but decided to hold my ground. Soon the dog appeared, an aging "lady dog," as my mother always called them. She waddled amiably across the road, sniffed attentively at the cuffs of my trousers, and wagged her rear quarters in the most friendly manner. Other encounters with dogs have not always been as happy. Along with postmen, photographers have something about them that antagonizes dogs. I've never had my trousers ripped off in New England, but this did happen in Italy, and my mirthful wife was witness to the mortifying episode.

In the early 1940's, when people were very spy-conscious, I encountered real difficulties. Housewives would look through their curtains, see me hiding under a mysterious black cloth with my camera, and decide that I might be an enemy agent. They would telephone the

The State Chamber, Jeremiah Lee
Mansion, Marblehead, Massachusetts, 1768,
from *Beyond New England Thresholds*

The Spiral Staircase, Gore Place,
Waltham, Massachusetts, 1804,
from *Beyond New England Thresholds*

THE BOWSPRITS OF THE FRIGATE "CONSTITUTION" AND THE "NANTUCKET"—CHARLESTOWN NAVY YARD

HISTORIC BOSTON
IN FOUR SEASONS

FANEUIL HALL

A CAMERA IMPRESSION

by SAMUEL CHAMBERLAIN

HASTINGS HOUSE *Publishers* NEW YORK

Frontispiece and title page of *Historic Boston,* one of the "American Landmarks" series

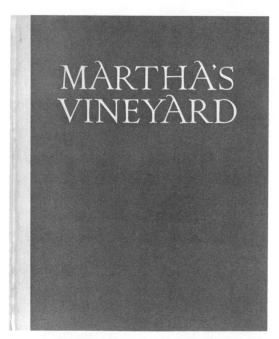

MARTHA'S VINEYARD

Martha's Vineyard, one of the ten
books in the "American Landmarks" series

police station. The next thing I knew a motorcycle cop would screech up to the scene, and ask what I was up to. This happened often enough so that I always carried my American passport for identification. Finally, however, I just gave up.

In 1938 we began a series of smaller, inexpensive gravure books, size 7¼ by 6 inches. Under the title of "American Landmarks," they were camera impressions of a few places most visited by summer tourists— Nantucket, Martha's Vineyard, Boston, Cambridge, Salem, Gloucester, Marblehead, Lexington and Concord, Portsmouth, and Longfellow's Wayside Inn. I designed each book, and made the handlettering for the jackets. Presented with an adequate introduction and captions, these little volumes approached in quality those found in Europe, and the response was good. A few of the books were set by hand in Garamond type by Elaine Rushmore at the Golden Hind Press, and they were quite distinctive for their modest price of a dollar and a quarter. Each of the ten books had photographic end papers, and in most cases the photographs were taken in all four seasons of the year. There is a certain historical quality to the pictures, for very few of them are encumbered by automobiles, and none of them show parking meters or television antennae, a situation that is rare indeed today. The American Landmarks books hummed along happily for years until rising printing costs made their price prohibitive.

My thanks are due to William Perry for a new etching opportunity that opened up in 1938. The active, one might say the "foraging"

The Raleigh Tavern, Williamsburg

partner of Perry, Shaw and Hepburn, the Boston architects, it was he who obtained an enviable commission for his firm, the rebuilding of Colonial Williamsburg, the ancient capitol of Virginia. Mr. Perry was convinced that etchings of the restored Williamsburg would be desirable, and negotiable if sold in the recently established Craft House. So I was invited to Williamsburg, and took a train through Virginia on a radiant spring day. It was my first glimpse of the South, and vastly exciting. Bela Norton, a displaced State o'Mainer, met me at the station, and installed me in a guest room at the Raleigh Tavern. A colored maid brought a hearty Virginia breakfast to the room every morning, and the days were spent happily in making pencil and pen-and-ink drawings of the old and restored buildings. The Governor's Palace, the newly rebuilt Capitol building, the Old Gaol and the Raleigh Tavern were all tempting subjects. But there were unrestored relics also—the Bruton Parish Church, the St. George Tucker House, the Apothecary's Shop and the dignified Semple House. All of them seemed adapted to the etching approach. Visitors were few at that early date, and sketching was a joy. In fact the Williamsburg interlude was a ray of pure sunshine, and I have been a fervent enthusiast for

St. George Tucker House, Williamsburg

103

Bruton Parish Church, Williamsburg

The Capitol, Williamsburg

The Palace Gardens, Williamsburg

The Chamberlains at Front Street,
Marblehead

this unique town from that day to this. The opportunity to design commemorative Wedgwood plates and to make an illustrated book on Williamsburg came within a few years, and only increased our affection for the ancient capitol and its gracious Virginian hosts.

Back in Marblehead we became impatient for a home of our own, and finally found a trim little pre-Revolutionary white house on Front Street. It had a gambrel-roofed top floor which we enlarged into a master's bedroom with bath. We also added a maid's wing, which turned out to be a providential move. Our furniture was rather sketchy, and we were wondering just what to do about it when a letter from France arrived. It was from Alexander and Brier Stoller, our old friends from the Paris days. They had found a commodious furnished villa on Cap Ferrat, overlooking the Mediterranean. "Why don't you come over and join us?" was the gist of the letter. Perhaps we were impetuous to leave our newly restored house, but we cabled back an enthusiastic acceptance. On the practical side, here was a chance to have my Williamsburg drypoints steel-faced in France and printed by the faithful Rigal.

We took a cabin for four on the *Conte di Savoia,* enjoyed an idyllic crossing, and were met in Cannes by the Stollers in their aging Packard. The car was impressive despite its years, and bore Dutch license plates. The French were impressed too, and we soon found that Lexi Stoller was known among them as "le richissime Hollandais." He was hard at work on a competition for the sculptured panel to be installed over the doorway of the Associated Press Building in Rockefeller Center, later won by Isamu Noguchi. The villa was huge, surrounded by terraces of cactus plants and persimmon trees, and there was a bright sunny room suitable for my etching studio. The third couple in the villa were Maestro Eugen Czenkar, the Hungarian symphony orchestra conductor, and his blonde German wife, Hermine. Our staff consisted of a cook, Madame Rossi, the cheerful plump Italian wife of the gardener, a small Italian cleaning girl, and Germaine Danloup, an energetic Frenchwoman who had been with us for a time in Senlis. A total lack of understanding between them was evident at once. But Madame Rossi's Italian dishes were delectable, and Germaine concealed her vexation behind an artificial smile. Life was most agreeable at Cap Ferrat. We bathed in the Mediterranean daily, joined a tennis club, and enjoyed our daily aperitifs on a sheltered terrace overlooking Villefranche harbor.

In spare time I managed to make two drypoints direct from nature. One was a view of the crowded Villefranche waterfront for a print club in New Haven. The other was a large plate of two rather shabby sailing vessels docked near the old fortress. Their sails hung limp from the masts, and made a rather exciting composition which was entitled "Mediterranean Wash Day." Ironically, at such a short distance from hostilities, both ships were Italian and were being loaded with French scrap iron destined for Italian steel plants.

During the summer I gathered six Williamsburg copper plates in a package, took an overnight train to Paris, and then a bus to Senlis. The faithful Fiat was waiting, and I sped to Fontenay-aux-Roses, where

Mediterranean Wash Day, Villefranche-sur-Mer

the reliable Edmond Rigal, more mournful than ever, pulled first states of my new drypoints. They were revised in his studio and after steel-facing in Paris were ready for final proofing. We spent hours establishing a "bon à tirer" of each plate, and then I drove the Fiat through Burgundy, paused for a delectable meal at the Hotel de la Poste in Beaune, and continued to the Riviera.

My second trip to Paris was far less tranquil. The clouds of war loomed over Europe in the autumn of 1938, and the tension caused by Hitler and his Nazis had all but paralyzed France. Paris was in a torment of apprehension as the four men of Europe met in Munich. My mission with Rigal seemed puny indeed, but I completed it, and managed to find a hard seat in a third class compartment back to Nice. The next day the news from Munich broke, and the world, in the words of a trusting soul from England, was ready for "peace in our time."

That autumn we enrolled the girls in a private school in Nice where Stephanie immediately distinguished herself by spilling a bag full of marbles on the stone floor of the chapel while Monseigneur was saying Mass. The *bonnes soeurs* couldn't have been nicer about it. By February I was obliged to return to MIT for the second semester, and alone took the bulky, oversized *Rex* on a tempestuous trip to New York.

The Market at Nice

Wedgwood plate of the Governor's Palace, Williamsburg

Finished drawing of St. George Tucker House, Williamsburg

Preliminary pencil sketch of The Capitol, Williamsburg

That winter I found comfortable quarters on Beacon Hill and walked daily to the Boston office of Perry, Shaw and Hepburn. Here a table by the window was mine to work on the drawings for a series of twelve commemorative dinner plates of Williamsburg. They were done in the style of old eighteenth-century engravings with idyllic clouds, romantic foliage treatment, flowery foregrounds and Colonial figures in costume. Twelve scenes, from modest cottages to the Governor's Palace, were studied first in pencil and later in detailed pen-and-ink. Once approved these were sent to England and engraved on copper by Wedgwood's highly skilled artists. The twelve dinner plates by Wedgwood appeared much later, after the war, and still find favor at the Craft House in Williamsburg.

Meanwhile, back in France, with the school year over, my wife took command of the Fiat and drove toward Paris, hoping to find passage back to America. In addition to the two little girls, Germaine, the French maid, was a passenger. We had asked her to come to Marblehead with us, and to our great surprise, she accepted with alacrity. She was a youngish spinster who had enjoyed countless American movies, and the prospect of seeing the land of Gary Cooper and Nelson Eddy enthralled her.

This was 1939, and transatlantic passages weren't picked up casually. Biscuit found accommodations on the *Ilsenstein,* but the trip was cancelled by Herr Hitler, and her space was transferred to the *Suffren.* This failed also, but finally a bus took them across Holland to Flushing and to the faithful old *Rotterdam,* which finally transported the little quartet to Hoboken, where I met them with a car and trailer. It was Sunday, and I parked without difficulty on Fifth Avenue in front of Childs Restaurant, where we introduced Germaine to waffles and chicken à la king. This was the beginning of her indoctrinization into the American scene. It was also the first step in my long-cherished ambition to write a book on the theme of a French cook installed in a rural American home.

There was news when we motored back to our little white house in Marblehead. We had new neighbors, none other than Arthur and Katherine Heintzelman. The noted portrait etcher, just back from France, had taken an apartment just next to us. A corridor just sixteen inches wide separated the two houses, enough for neighborly exchanges, but a problem for putting out the trash barrels. The Marblehead Arts Association lost no time in making Mr. Heintzelman its president, and his influence was evident at once.

By the following June, for a day at least, Marblehead became the print center of America. To honor Frank W. Benson, the dean of American etchers who lived in nearby Salem, the local arts association arranged a retrospective exhibition of ninety Benson prints, mostly of his famous wild fowl. This marked his twenty-fifth year as an etcher, and called for a special show of affection from his fellow printmakers. Mr. Benson made his first etching, a view of Salem Harbor, in 1882, but did not take up the etching profession until many years later.

Five graphic artists gathered in the old King Hooper Mansion, the home of a prosperous merchant shipper in Colonial days, and demon-

Frank W. Benson watching Kerr Eby print an etching at the King Hooper House, Marblehead
(photograph by Donald Gellatly, June, 1940)

strated the art of the copperplate medium to an audience that poured
into Marblehead from Boston and the North Shore. John Taylor Arms
brought his etching press from Greenfield Hill and demonstrated the
art of pure etching as only he could do it. He cleaned the plate, waxed
it, smoked it and needled it with both hands, never stopping his
stentorian monologue for an instant. While his enthralled audience
watched breathessly he protected the plate with stopping out varnish,
bit it in several immersions of acid, cleaned it, and triumphantly
printed a proof before his time had run out. At the conclusion his
listeners were limp with exhaustion, but he was as fresh as ever. John
Arms deserved top billing in the third-floor ballroom, and received it.
Each of the other print makers occupied an old paneled room in the

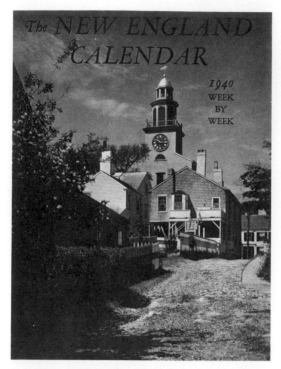

Nantucket, Massachusetts
Cover of the first *New England Calendar*, 1940

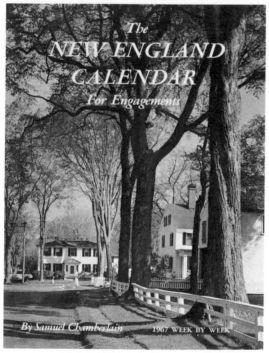

Kennebunkport, Maine
Cover of the *New England Calendar*, 1967

mansion and showed his specialty. Arthur Heintzelman made a dry-point of a round-faced little boy who sat patiently in a chair. Thomas Nason, the gifted engraver from Connecticut, executed a delicate copper engraving, and I made a soft ground etching of the King Hooper Mansion itself. For a plate printer, we had the very best, none other than Kerr Eby, whose dramatic etchings of World War I had made him famous. He pulled prints from all four demonstration plates under the friendly gaze of Frank Benson and the popping flashlights of Boston news photographers. That June day in Marble-head was one to remember!

A new experiment in gravure printing was initiated with Hastings House in 1939. Gathering together fifty-five vertical photographs of the beauties of New England, I laid out the first *New England Calendar,* a week-by-week engagement book. A calendar page for each week had spaces to inscribe morning, afternoon and evening engagements, and facing it was a nostalgic photograph of a New England subject. The calendar for 1940 sold for a dollar, and did so well that two extra printings were needed before Christmas. There was nothing else like it on the market. The next spring I made a pilgrimage to Virginia to create a *Virginia Calendar* for 1941. Both of these calendars have now passed the quarter-century mark, and still carry on in spite of very strenuous competition. So does the *California Calendar,* illustrated by varied western photographers. My format and idea were imitated by other publishers, and there are now weekly engagement calendars on kittens, puppies, horses, flower arrangements, colleges and gardens. In most recent years our daughter Narcisse dreamed up engagement calendars dealing with French, Italian and American cooking. This was a family affair with Narcisse doing the editing, while her mother translated and adapted the recipes, and I furnished the photographs. These later appeared in book form, and gave the reader a pictorial trip through each country with some two hundred and twenty recipes as well. Reprints from the New England and Virginia calendars were also made, and there are now seven books, illustrated in gravure, that originally made their debut as calendars: *Ever New England, Springtime in Virginia, The Flavor of France* (Volumes I and II), *The Flavor of Italy, The Sampler of American Cooking,* and *The New England Scene.* We have recently added a *Calendar of Antiques* to the list.

With Germaine settled in her wing of our old house in Marblehead, life took on a new amplitude. The combination of a happy existence in a yachting community, embellished by French cooking, was something special. Germaine was a gifted cook, not as fine as our faithful Francine perhaps, but she transformed the basic fundamentals from Marblehead's butcher shop, fish store and supermarket into authentic, aromatic French dishes that brought joy to our epicurean family. She spoke not a word of English, so one of us always accompanied her on her shopping missions. Invariably a few anecdotes accumulated with each trip, and it soon became evident that we had here a theme for a series of articles, and perhaps a book as well.

The Wine Merchant's House, La Charité-sur-Loire, reproduced in "Burgundy at a Snail's Pace,"
Gourmet, January, 1941

I had very definite ideas about where the articles should be published
—in a then unborn magazine called *Gourmet*. This happened to be the
case, because, a few years before, a tall, distinguished Bostonian named
Earle MacAusland had come to my dingy studio in the Rogers Building and discussed his editorial ambitions. The lack of an American
magazine on gastronomy troubled him, and he announced his intention of launching "Gourmet, The Magazine of Good Living." He
sounded me out on the idea of becoming the editor, but I am just as
glad that I declined, since the rate of mortality among the editors has
been rather high. He also invited me to send in contributions, and it
was here that I began to visualize stories of our two cooks, Francine
and Germaine, and their impact on our French and American house-
holds. By resorting to a little fiction I was able to combine the two
personalities into one.

The articles appeared as "Clementine in the Kitchen" and were
written under the *nom de plume* of Phineas Beck, an anglicization of

"Chez Léon,"
from *Clementine in the Kitchen*

Clementine's Kitchen

here the cheerful Clémentine reigned

Our Cordon Bleu Clémentine

Our Cordon Bleu, Clementine

Drawings by Henry Stahlhut, from *Clementine in the Kitchen*

Village Wine Merchant, Burgundy

fin bec which, in French, denotes a gourmet with a fine nose for food and wine. It was great fun to write them because they were ninety per cent true. The episode with Francine and the snails when she captured them and put them in cardboard shoe boxes, only to have them escape and climb over the kitchen ceiling, was totally true. Germaine's vexing adventures with the unyielding Yankee grocer and the butcher who refused to cut her thin *escalopes* were entirely accurate. On a trip with us to coastal Maine she discovered great clusters of mussels on the rocks, which she prepared with herbs and white wine to the enchantment of our hosts. This made refreshing gastronomic prose, and *Gourmet* accepted my first chapter.

When the inaugural issue of the magazine appeared in January, 1941, it led off with my article on "Burgundy at a Snail's Pace," illustrated by a pencil drawing of a steep-roofed wine merchant's house in La Charité-sur-Loire. "Clementine in the Kitchen" made her debut in the February issue and ran continuously for almost two years. When it came time to combine all these chapters in a book, I added a partly fictitious ending in which Clemintine married a French-Canadian widower with two spindly children. Henry Stalhut, *Gourmet's* cover artist, made humorous pen-and-ink drawings to accompany my illus-

The Gambrel-roofed Cottage in New England, from *Clementine in the Kitchen*

trations, and Biscuit assembled a toothsome collection of French recipes purporting to be "Extracts from Clementine's Notebook." Published in October, 1943, by Hastings House in cooperation with
Gourmet, Clementine in the Kitchen has made many friends, and is
now in her tenth printing.

With the outbreak of hostilities in Europe and the first months of
the "phoney war," a natural uneasiness came over our pro-French
household. We joined French war relief organizations and contributed what we could. With the fall of France in 1940, a more urgent
mood descended, and I decided to attempt a new book that would fill
the double purpose of building up affection for France and raising
funds for the admirable French war relief organization then functioning in America. Our close friend Donald Moffat offered to write the
introduction and to help in various other ways. With the backing of
this dedicated Francophile assured, I embarked on a pictorial essay
on La Belle France under the title, *France Will Live Again,* "The
Portrait of a Peaceful Interlude (1919-1939)." Using my own prints,
drawings and photographs, a layout was made dividing the beauties of
France into pictorial chapters. Some concerned French villages, towns,
churches and cathedrals. Others portrayed the shore line of France,

Trie Château,
from *France Will Live Again*

The Manoir d'Ango near Dieppe, from *France Will Live Again*

A Farm at Cousnicourt (Oise), from *France Will Live Again*

The Sunlit Tower, Colmar, from *France Will Live Again*

The Abandoned Château, from *France Will Live Again*

The Farm Gate, from *France Will Live Again*

and her peaceful countryside with farms, cottages, *manoirs* and châteaux, with an intention to create a maximum of affection for the martyred country. Walter Frese of Hastings House undertook to print the book in sheet-fed gravure, and to make a most generous sales arrangement with the French war relief group. Donald Moffat and I both offered our royalties for the same purpose, and *France Will Live Again* appeared in December, 1940. It carried a nostalgic watercolor of Senlis on its jacket, and met with an encouraging response that called for several reprintings.

In the meantime, a message from George Macy, creator and president of the Limited Editions Club, brought me to New York. This bold, erudite and daring little man had built up a small empire among American bibliophiles, and his publications were the ultimate in fine bookmaking. We had luncheon together at his favorite table in the Oak Room of the Plaza, and at the conclusion of this pleasant formality I had a commission to illustrate *The Education of Henry Adams*

The Adams Mansion, Quincy

Mount Vernon Street, Boston

From *The Education of Henry Adams*

with original etchings. This remarkable book, the autobiography of a most distinguished and quite mysterious New Englander, was rich in descriptive passages that lent themselves well to illustration. Another encouraging fact was that the book was to be designed and printed by Daniel Berkeley Updike of the Merrymount Press in Boston. Here was a master printer and book designer whom I had always admired, and getting to know him was an auxiliary reward.

Quite a long time was spent in working up the twelve sketches for the final etching illustrations. Some of them were pure New England subjects such as Boston's Beacon Street in the snow and Mount Vernon Street in early spring. The Adams Mansion in Quincy, Harvard Yard and Wadsworth House in Cambridge were all discussed in the text. Henry Adams' affection for Rome, London, and particularly France, was reflected in etchings of Ara Coeli in Rome, the Houses of Parliament in London and, of course, views of Mont St. Michel and Chartres. The twelve etchings were bitten in iron perchloride, which gives more delicacy than nitric acid. They were small plates, most of them measuring 6¾ by 4⅜ inches, and a few of them were fortified with aquatint. They were steel-faced and printed by hand in the shop of Charles Furth in New York. At that time Mr. Furth had enough hand presses

Harvard Yard, from *The Education of Henry Adams*

117

The North Porch of the Virgin of Chartres   The Town of Chartres

From *The Education of Henry Adams*

Wadsworth House, Cambridge,
from *The Education of Henry Adams*

and veteran plate printers to pull editions of 1,500 impressions from the twelve plates. Today it would be out of the question. They were dry-wiped prints without *retroussage,* but they had a certain warmth, especially the ones with aquatint.

The book was printed in Times Roman, a typeface especially imported from England by Mr. Updike. It is a handsome book, and a glowing tribute to the great New England master printer and designer. It appeared in February, 1942 (a few months after Updike's death), and later in a much larger edition of the Heritage Club.

With France occupied by the Nazis, it was Britain that bore the brunt of the struggle in 1941. In our limited way, Donald Moffat and I set out to assemble a book that would draw attention to Britain and the treasures she was fighting to protect. This was a very different book from its French predecessor, since it called upon any number of English, Scottish and American printmakers and photographers to contribute the illustrations. These did not have to be sent from Europe. They were already assembled in the collections of the Library of Congress, the Metropolitan Museum of Art and the New York Public Library. I spent several weeks in Washington and New York, choosing the prints and having them photographed. Then came the matter

artists Proof II/V   Samuel Chamberlain

Essex Village, from *This Realm, This England*

of writing each artist and obtaining permission to use his work. This was a fascinating pursuit, for it put me in touch with the greatest of contemporary etchers. It was a joy to correspond with Sir D. Y. Cameron, Sir Muirhead Bone, Sir Frank Short, James McBey, William Walcot, Francis Dodd, Henry Rushbury, Frank Brangwyn, Robert Austin, and many others.

Since our proceeds for the proposed book were all to go to the British War Relief Society, the response from each artist was invariably affirmative, and the friendly letters they sent have always been treasured. Prints by Seymour Haden, Joseph Pennell, James McNeill Whistler, F. L. Griggs, and even old John Sell Cotman also appeared in the book, but it was too late to ask their permission. Among the Americans, Louis Rosenberg, Kerr Eby and John Arms all contributed fine prints, and I contributed several of my own drypoints and photographs.

Butcher Row, Coventry
Frontispiece of *This Realm, This England*

When it appeared late in 1941 the book was almost a catalogue of great British prints. It was called *This Realm, This England,* and its chapters dealt with the beauty of Britain—London, English villages, towns and cities, the countryside, coast and rivers, castles and cathedrals. Donald Moffat wrote a stirring introduction, and the book was something of an emotional triumph, as well as a modest fund-raiser. Gravure printing did full justice to the prints which, besides the masters of yesterday, embrace younger British artists who are in their prime today.

About this time came an offer from the Joseph Dixon Crucible Company to make pencil drawings of historic landmarks in England and

Church of St. Vulfran, Abbeville

Courtyard of the Temple, London

the continent that had been bombed or otherwise destroyed during World War II. This was an advertising assignment with artistic appeal, and I made up twelve full-page Eldorado pencil drawings in all. They appeared in architectural and art magazines, and later in folders for students of pencil technique, and hopefully may have had some propaganda value. The fine old timbered St. Peter's Hospital, bombed out in Bristol, made a good sketch subject, and so did the brick courtyard of the Temple in London. The martyred Town Hall in Middleburg, Holland, the church of St. Vulfran in Abbeville, France, and the church of St. Laurens in Rotterdam were others in the Continental series. Adjoining each pencil drawing was a description of the technique employed. In most cases, the body of the drawing was made with softer pencils ranging from B to 4B, and kept as sharp as possible. Middle tones were supplied by harder pencils sharpened to a wedge shape. Finally, wash effects similar to a wash drawing were achieved by using a hard pencil such as a 4H which had been worn to a wide, smooth, flat surface. In each case, a maximum pressure was applied to the pencil in this technique, and breakage was frequent.

The attack on Pearl Harbor and the immediate involvement of our country in the war seemed to justify a third volume, seeking to portray the beauty of America and to demonstrate that here too was something worth fighting for. This turned out to be primarily a book of photographs, although American printmakers contributed many woodcuts and etchings. To obtain a photographic cross section of this whole vast country, I went through the voluminous files of photographic sources in New York, such as Ewing Galloway, and corresponded with camera clubs with good success. Famed photographers such as Francis Benjamin Johnston, Josef Muench and Ray Atkeson opened up their portfolios, and any number of fine pictures turned up in the files of the Farm Security Administration in Washington. Months were needed to assemble this pictorial bounty into a book. It embraced the majesty of the plains and the Far West, as well as the more familiar themes of the South, New England, the seacoast and the Great Lakes. Thomas W. Nason contributed several wood engravings, while Stow Wengenroth sent some of his superb lithographs. Among the other American printmakers were Frank W. Benson, Kerr Eby, Alfred Hutty, Childe Hassam, Armin Landeck and John H. Winkler. Several of my own prints and photographs were also used. It was a handsome volume when it appeared in July, 1942, with the title *Fair Is Our Land,* "The Portrait of America." There is a certain timeless quality to this collection of graphic Americana, and today, a quarter of a century later, the book still seems entirely contemporary and full of life.

Even though our country was immersed in war on two fronts, old retreads such as Don Moffat and Sam Chamberlain were not greatly in demand. He obtained a commission in the Navy, however, while my application was turned down. Luckily the United States Army Air Force was more hospitable, and in September I was commissioned a captain and sent to the Officers Training School in Miami Beach.

Bend in the Road, Newcastle, New Hampshire, from *Fair is Our Land*

Here life had several good aspects. We luxuriated in rooms at the Roney Plaza at a dollar a day. The restaurant food was lamentable, but the weather was warm and the beaches tempting. We rose at dawn, and the ensuing hours of classes and calisthenics were long and strenuous. The waistlines of our delegation of middle-aged executives reduced perceptibly on the sun-drenched drill field before the four weeks were up.

Then a group of us were sent to the Air Force Intelligence School in Harrisburg, Pennsylvania, where we were indoctrinated in the fundamentals of combat and photographic intelligence. After elaborate graduation ceremonies, we were shipped to Atlantic City where we occupied rather derelict hotels, stripped of furniture, to await shipment overseas. There was time for a happy family reunion in Boston, followed by exasperating weeks of waiting in the New Jersey resort. Finally our small group was shipped to Fort Hamilton in New York, where our contingent of twelve officers and a graying civilian was loaded in a motor ship called the *Doña Aniceta*. She had been built in Italy, but sailed under the Philippine flag and had a Philippine captain, crew, and—alas—cook. At six knots an hour we joined a convoy headed toward the Panama Canal, where we tied up for almost a week. This permitted a bit of exploration in Colon before the ship steamed through the Canal and then headed southward along the Pacific coast of South America.

Time dragged for the next few weeks. The *Doña Aniceta* was a freighter charged with a hot cargo, and although it had six cabins and a lounge, the deck space was limited to one narrow alley exactly seven-

Duke of Gloucester Street, Williamsburg, from *Fair is Our Land*

Gateway in Cairo

Cairo

teen paces long. We took turns on this morning promenade, and played poker and shuffleboard for substantial stakes. In an attempt to do something constructive, I joined Lieutenant Arthur Giuliani, an ex-member of the New York narcotic squad, in swapping language lessons. I taught him French, and he tutored me in Italian. This came in handy later. We could see Cape Horn in the distance as the ship turned toward the south Atlantic, and churned through the Roaring Forties. By the time we had rounded the Horn, we were so accustomed to the tossing of the ship that nobody was seasick on the month-long trek to the Cape of Good Hope. The refrigerator went bad midway, and all fish, meat and vegetables had to be tossed overboard. We lived on tinned food after that, and it proved to be a relief after the slovenly efforts of the Philippine cook.

In Durban, South Africa, we had a week of repose in a comfortable hotel while the ship had her valves ground, or something of the sort. War seemed remote indeed in Durban. The serene life of the British colonial, with his tennis clubs, bowling greens and tea lounges was something of a surprise. We also had more than a glimpse of Apartheid. We rejoined the ship to find that a new refrigeration plant had been installed, and sailed northward past Madagascar to Aden, the hottest community I have ever encountered. There were some fine sketch subjects here, but I didn't have the stamina. All I wanted was an iced drink. Small wonder that Aden is considered a hardship post by the British! With a sigh of relief we sailed through the Red Sea and reached the Suez Canal. By the time we arrived at our destination, Suez, the trip from New York had consumed exactly seventy-five days.

Our small quota of photo interpreters was transported to Heliopolis, a few miles from Cairo. The name meant little to me except that I recalled vaguely that it had once been the home of Pearl White, the heroine of "The Perils of Pauline." Sure enough, her villa was still in evidence, the most flamboyant and rococo of all the tortuous architecture that lingered in the town. In Heliopolis we were assigned to a photo-reconnaissance unit that worked in close cooperation with British photo interpreters. After a stiff indoctrination course, I was assigned to "Shipping." My commanding officer was Flying Officer Perkins, who turned out to be a slightly plump and most pleasant English girl. She was rather strict, however, and frowned fiercely if I opened my morning mail when it arrived at eight, rather than waiting for the tea break at ten. When some enterprising British officer invited her for a spot of tennis, she would respond in military code, which impressed me very much indeed. She put me to work scanning air photographs of the Grecian islands, and soon I felt a close kinship with Chios and its windmills, Santorin and its steep hillside ascent, Rhodes, Mytilene, Minos and many another Aegean island. More important was the assignment to report daily on the shipping situation in Piraeus, the seaport of Athens. There was plenty of activity here, but the port was not molested.

Life in Heliopolis was agreeable in spite of the relentless heat. We worked from eight in the morning to eight at night, but there was a

CAIRO

Slums of Cairo

BANKS OF THE NILE

Banks of the Nile, Egypt

Coptic Church, Egypt

four-hour siesta daily, from one to five. On Saturday afternoons and Sundays the war was called off for photo interpreters, and only the sentries were on duty. This provided a wonderful chance to make sketches of Cairo, and I rarely failed to take a tram into the city with my sketchpad and collapsible stool. The subject matter was irresistible, although the curiosity of the encircling Egyptians all but blocked it from view. I have one sketch of the fortified gates of the city that was never finished because the ground area was continually blocked by gaping Egyptians. The mosques, the multistoried tenements, the shops and the streets of Cairo all made tempting subjects. So did the villages along the banks of the Nile and vistas of the pyramids screened in palm trees. I made a small portfolio of Egyptian drawings, intending some day to transform them into etchings. Sadly enough, they never got beyond the drawing stage.

Our group of some fifteen American officers lived in a large one-story villa with high ceilings and voluminous net curtains to keep out the flies. A staff of six Egyptians took care of the household. The kitchen brigade was headed by a brigand named Mohammed whose meals were tasteless and skimpy, despite the respectable per diem contribution of each officer. I protested much too loudly, with the inevitable result. "Captain, as of now, you are the mess officer," bluntly announced our major in command. He gave me a jeep for marketing, and authority to spend the food budget that formerly had rested in Mohammed's slippery fingers. The gastronomic picture did improve,

Ancient Archways in Cairo

The Poultry Man's Shop, Heliopolis, Egypt

and beef was served now and then instead of emaciated goat. Wine and beer were introduced at the evening meal with pronounced success, and I sought out unusual products when possible.

This brings up a rather remarkable poultry store that we passed four times a day walking to and from work. It was an intriguing little shop, framed in delicately carved stonework, and filled with wooden cages containing every sort of edible fowl—pigeons, chickens, ducks, pheasant and, best of all, a magnificent turkey. The owner of the shop had his own efficient way of feeding his birds. Instead of placing a pan of grain in their cages, he made up a larger container of mash, a mysterious combination of grain and other ingredients. Filling his own mouth with this mash, he would seize each bird, pry its beak open, and force the nourishment down its throat. It looked rather cruel, but the birds seemed to like it. My fellow officers, however, were appalled and disgusted and considered the whole thing most unsanitary. That beautiful turkey, however, continued to catch my fancy. I made a drawing of the shop in siesta time, and became acquainted with the owner. When not engaged in his feeding chores he was a personable fellow, and spoke a little French. Later, when we received orders to transfer to Tunisia, I arranged a final dinner in the villa, featuring a good French wine and a noble eggplant dish. The *pièce de résistance* was a beautiful turkey weighing eighteen pounds, stuffed with chestnuts and accompanied by a rich, aromatic sauce. It made a sensation as

Sidi-Bou-Saïd, Tunis

The Hillside, Sidi-Bou-Saïd, Tunisia

The Hilltop Bazaar, Sidi-Bou-Saïd, Tunisia

Major Pollock carved it with skill, and the servants passed the plates around the table. Soon compliments began to come my way. "Where on earth did you find this wonderful bird?" was the consensus. I demurely said nothing. Then the truth slowly began to break. The faces of my fellow officers began to cloud, and before I suffered bodily insult and injury, I stole out into the night.

The next day we were flown to Tunisia, where our headquarters were in the little Arab hill town of Sidi Bou Saïd, not far from ancient Carthage. It was a summer retreat for wealthy Tunisians, and had several sumptuous villas that sheltered the top military brass at that point in the North African campaign. During our stay President Roosevelt stopped overnight on a secret mission and was met by Generals Eisenhower, Spaatz, Bedell Smith, Norstad, and many another *grosse légume,* as the French have a way of saying.

This little Arab town was full of sketch subjects, too—bazaars, mosques, minarets, Arab cafés and strange sunbaked houses with semicylindrical roofs. As a consequence I often devoted a part of the two-hour lunch period to pencil drawing. This led to a lucky break for me, as one of the British officers who looked over my shoulder was Major Tim Ashby, a dashing fellow who was looking for an artist— for a special assignment. Photo interpreters have a difficult task scanning aerial photographs with a stereoscope, and sometimes make glaring mistakes in identifying gun emplacements, road blocks, pill boxes, and anti-aircraft positions. Major Ashby wanted somebody who could sketch, measure and photograph these enemy defenses after they had been captured, and then make illustrated reports that would help the photo interpreters in their delicate task. We had a meeting with

126

Reflected Light, Sidi-Bou-Saïd

Colonel Elliott Roosevelt, then the commanding officer, who wrote out the directive for a very choice assignment. I was given a crack photographic expert, Sergeant Paul Pelech, and flown from the Tunisian airport of Le Marsa to Pomigliano d'Arco, an airport a few miles inland from Naples. This was shortly after the Salerno landings, and southern Italy was in a chaotic state.

I was issued a new jeep and a 4 x 5 Army Speed Graphic camera with a tripod, all the fixings, and quantities of film. Then we waited for the rain to stop. We lived in the Pomigliano village schoolhouse with a group of British photo interpreters and shared their morbid meals. When the weather lifted, Pelech and I struck out with our jeep and made photographs and drawings of the gun emplacements and pill boxes along the Autostrada south of Naples that had long puzzled the photo interpreters. At night, in the schoolhouse, I would make the finished drawings and write a report in strictly military English, without a single vagrant adjective. These were amplified by Pelech's pictures, and the whole report was photographed on expensive paper supplied by Uncle Sam, giving it a fine luxurious luster.

The Arched Passageway, Sidi-Bou-Saïd

127

Farmyard at Licignano di Napoli, Italy

The author sharing *minestra* with a
favorite Italian family in Pomigliano d'Arco

Having a jeep meant that I could take occasional trips to nearby Naples in off hours, and my roommate in the schoolhouse, Major Frank Elworthy, joined me in many shopping expeditions. The shops in this sprawling city were often pathetically bare, but a careful buyer could find some good coral and costume jewelry for his womenfolk at home. I began to haunt the second-hand bookshops, newly opened after years of hibernation. In one of them was a treasure, the complete culinary library of a French chef who had apparently worked in Naples at one time. There were over thirty volumes, many of them classics, and I made a deal for the lot in occupation dollars. Sending them home was no problem. Once securely wrapped in numerous parcels, they could be sent at domestic postal rates by the Army Post Office. Several fine Italian cookbooks were in the same shop, and today they are among the treasures of my gastronomic library.

This was about my closest approach to the epicurean arts during the long stay in southern Italy. The food situation there was forlorn, and we subsisted on army rations entirely. There was one memorable exception to the usual run of mediocre cooking when, on a sunny day, a few of us Americans were invited to luncheon at a French officers' mess in the town of Venafro. Here we were enchanted to find a reasonable facsimile of a classic French meal, beginning with hors d'oeuvre of radishes, cauliflower *au vinaigrette,* and a *pâté* based on finely

128

An Archway in Campania, Pomigliano d'Arco

ROADBLOCK AT CERCOLA
Map Ref. GSGS-4229 Sh.184/I-304509

Report No.7

Roadblock at Cercola, from a report on enemy defences

Vesuvius in Eruption, March, 1944

ground and seasoned Vienna sausages straight from the G. I. commissary. The *pièce de résistance* was a delicious small individual cabbage for each diner, stuffed with aromatic chopped beef. There was a fairly good white wine to accompany this unexpected splendor. Afterwards I asked to be allowed to congratulate the chef who had accomplished this culinary feat, and met a genial, youngish man who, not surprisingly, had worked in a good Paris restaurant. I asked the secret of his stuffed cabbages and he explained that, first of all, the young heads had been liberated from a cabbage patch in the abandoned town. The stuffing was achieved by opening numerous cans of a melancholy C ration called Meat and Beans. "What I do, *mon commandant*," he explained in French, "is to empty the contents on my work table. Then with a knife I push the *bayonz* to one side and the *mayott* to the other. Soon I have enough *mayott* to make a *farce,* with plenty of seasoning. *Voici mon secret.*"

130

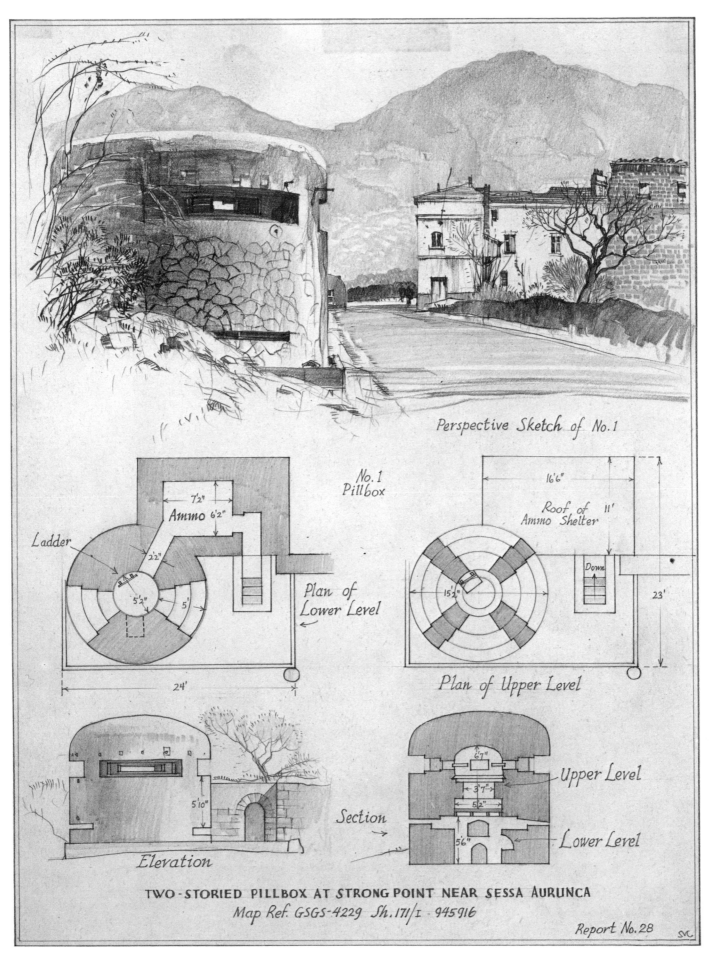

Perspective Sketch of No.1

No. 1
Pillbox

Ammo 7'2" 6'2"

Ladder

Roof of
Ammo Shelter 11'

2'2"

5'2" 5'

16'6"

Down

15'2"

Plan of
Lower Level

24'

Plan of Upper Level

23'

Upper Level

6'7"

3'7"

5'2"

Lower Level

5'10"

5'6"

Elevation

Section

TWO-STORIED PILLBOX AT STRONG POINT NEAR SESSA AURUNCA
Map Ref. GSGS-4229 Sh.171/I · 945916

Report No. 28

Two-storied Pillbox at strongpoint near Sessa Aurunca, from a report on enemy defenses

Isola Tiberina, Rome, early June, 1944

Piccola Marina, Capri

It was a long, rainy and exciting winter. Pomigliano lay at the base of Mount Vesuvius, and when the great volcano indulged in its last eruption in March, 1944, we had a balcony seat, and made many sensational photographs. As the winter wore on, we came to know the devastated Cassino area and the Hitler Line, and then the pitifully exposed Anzio sector. When "Anzio Annie," the famous concealed long-range gun on railway carriages, was finally captured, we recorded it on film and labored mightily with the tape measure.

About this time I was given a major's oak leaves and Sergeant Pelech had new hash marks on his sleeve. Rome was next in line, and we drove our jeep with the triumphant motorcade into Rome on June 5, 1944. This second fall of Rome appeared to us to be a big day in history, but the event was almost totally ignored. The Normandy landings the next day completely stole the headlines. Our last assignment was to cover the French invasion and capture of Elba on June 17, 1944, and it was a thriller. After this was recorded in a lengthy report, our assignment was about complete. We had produced seventy-six reports filling three thick volumes, and as a generous reward, we both were decorated with the Legion of Merit.

One adventure remained for us, a visit to Romania to evaluate the damage caused by American 15th Air Force air raids on the oil refineries of Ploesti. This much-publicized and in some ways quite tragic expedition had left many unanswered questions. With the sudden departure of the German forces, it was a race between the Russians and their allies, the Americans, to see who got there first. We flew several B-17's from Bari, in Italy, and landed the first contingent of officers, but the Russians followed in force. In the Ambassador Hotel in Bucharest we were a cluster of twenty Americans in an avalanche of over 800 Russians.

When our team of investigators drove to Ploesti and tried to visit the damaged refineries, we were rebuffed by Russian sentries who blocked every attempt to get through the gates. This was an early taste of the Russian intransigence that has since become one of the hard facts of life. Only when we flew in a three-star general who outranked the Russians were we able to visit the refineries and assess the bomb damage. Our photographic team worked valiantly to record the destruction, which was hideous beyond belief.

Back in the Royal Palace in Caserta, the Allied Headquarters outside Naples, I prepared a voluminous photographic report on Ploesti. The pictures were dramatic enough, but I found so much twisted steel, shattered pipes and pools of black oil most distasteful. It was the ugliest publication I have ever issued. The big brass liked it, however, and General Eaker pinned a Bronze Star on my tunic.

In February, 1945 I left a chilly tent in Caserta and was flown to London to join the United States Strategic Bombing Survey. This was a rather abrupt change, especially in regard to housing. Thanks to Lend Lease, I occupied a well-heated double room with bath in the distinguished old Hyde Park Hotel. Every morning I walked across the park for breakfast at Grosvenor House, where an officers' mess known as Willow Run was installed.

My assignment was to reproduce voluminous reports on bomb damage in Germany, written by inspection teams, in a series of uniform publications. I was given a detachment of thirty-five noncoms who were supposedly proficient at typing, map making and lettering. Of all the corporals and sergeants in the group, one had more energy, skill and imagination than the others. This was Corporal Ruth Krenz, a rural Nebraska banker's daughter who had passed the Civil Service exams in Washington and had become a Verityper expert. I lost no time in getting her another stripe and making her my deputy. Photography played a part also, and the faithful Sergeant Pelech was a member of the team. Buses took us daily from London to Bushy Park, near Hampton Court, and here the bound reports were produced. It was a bookmaking job, and rather dull. My sole artistic contribution to the Survey was to hand-letter a certificate to be awarded to its members.

Big Ben, London, 1945

National Gallery and St. Martins-
in-the-Fields, London, 1945

UNITED STATES
STRATEGIC BOMBING SURVEY
THIS is to certify that
served as a member of the United States Strategic Bombing
Survey in the European Theatre of Operations from____
194   to   194
In appreciation of his conscientious and able perform-
ance of duty to his country this Certificate is awarded
with commendation and grateful appreciation.
DATE:
                    FRANKLIN D'OLIER, Chairman.

Hand-lettered certificate, 1945

King's College, Cambridge, 1945

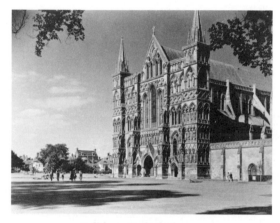
Salisbury Cathedral, 1945

Falstaff Hotel, Canterbury, 1945

Still, it was adventurous to be in London in wartime, and the visits of V1 and V2 bombs made it more so. Week ends were free, and I usually made the best of them by taking a train or bus to some picturesque English town. Thus I had chances to sketch and photograph Canterbury, Winchester, Oxford, Cambridge, Salisbury and many another celebrated place during the long months that followed. The highlight of the London experience, of course, was the celebration of VE Day. We joined the immense throng that gathered in front of Buckingham Palace and watched King George VI, Queen Elizabeth and the two little princesses appear over and over again on the balcony, wildly applauded by the throng. Finally another figure joined them, the solid and triumphant Winston Churchill. That was a moment one never forgets!

In the calm interlude that followed, I was authorized a week's leave in Paris, in order to visit our long-neglected house in Senlis. The exchange was ferociously against the dollar at that time, and I was lucky to be able to frequent the Allied Officer's Club on the Place St. Augustin for GI nourishment at a reasonable stipend. A good French restaurant meal cost a fortune. Transportation was another hopeless problem, but I took the Metro to the Porte de la Villette, and then hitchhiked on American military vehicles at will. Our old house was almost intact, although the roof had been punctured in places by fragments of antiaircraft shells, and it leaked badly. Neighbors related the story. The dashing lieutenant colonel who rented our house was killed during the first weeks of the war. His languorous mistress lingered on in the house for some time, but left in midwinter, neglecting to turn off the water. The pipes froze, and when our neighbors saw water flowing out under the front door, they called our agent who found the cellar flooded and six inches of water on the ground floor, not at all good for the furniture or the lowest shelf of books. The house was then turned over to a Belgian who had been bombed out. His German wife gave French lessons to German soldiers who were billeted in the town. After lesson time, they were in the habit of taking away a book or a *bibelot,* or a small piece of furniture as a souvenir. The house looked stripped and forlorn. News of my arrival spread rapidly, it would appear, for soon I was honored by a visit from Monsieur le Percepteur, who presented a bill for some $450 in back taxes. Everything considered, it was a rather melancholy homecoming.

The next few weeks in London were anticlimactic, and time dragged for the soldier waiting to be sent home. I amused myself by haunting the secondhand bookshops again, looking for epicurean tomes. In one shop off Bond Street was a beautifully bound six-volume set of *Le Cuisinier Moderne* by Vincent de la Chapelle, an early eighteenth-century master chef. I gazed at it longingly, but decided that it was too expensive. The book dealer's answer to the problem was not exactly typical. "Take it home with you, sir," he suggested. "Here's the bill. Just pay me when you can."

At that time London restaurants and hotels were still obliged to produce a three-course meal for five shillings, although there were ingenious ways of adding extras for music, cover, service and other

Old Nassau Hall, Princeton

The Palace Gates, Williamsburg,
from *Behold Williamsburg*

Mount Vernon, 1946,
from *Mount Vernon, A Handbook*

things. It was a novel experience to dine cheaply at the Savoy or the Café Royal, and I put in a bit of gastronomic research, sometimes rather forlorn, on many autumn evenings.

It was a long wait, but I was finally flown back in a bucket-seat transport plane to New York in late October, 1945. On November 3 I was relieved of active duty at the Pentagon, and was a civilian once again, ready to face the inspector of Internal Revenue.

Back in the little white house on Front Street it was evident that Time had indeed galloped along. Narcisse was in her senior year at Bennington, and Stephanie was in a preparatory school high in the New Hampshire hills. My energetic wife had spent the war years in Boston running The Caledonian Market for the benefit of the British War Relief Society. Among the unopened letters, a pleasant bit of news was waiting. The National Academy of Design had promoted me to Academician in April, 1945. The American Academy of Arts and Sciences had elected me to fellowship on May first of the same year.

The accumulation of untended chores and unanswered mail was appalling. My most urgent need was for a studio, and I found one over Osborne's grocery store located at Marblehead's principal crossroads. The room had once been a newspaper printing plant, and could easily accommodate the etching press, cabinets, bookcases and tables that I had shipped out from my old studio in MIT. The walls were rather bare, and I lost little time in covering them with large Piranesi and Decaris engravings. The only drawback was a steep flight of twenty-three steps that had to be climbed, and of course they seemed to get steeper as the years went by.

Among the unanswered letters was one that was particularly welcome. It came from a great bibliophile and print collector, Elmer Adler. He wanted me to visit his Print Center in Princeton and give a talk to his students. All printmakers admired this dedicated man, who was an enormous influence in the graphic arts, and I accepted with enthusiasm. Out of this winter trip to Princeton came an invitation to make a drypoint of Old Nassau Hall, so dear to the heart of every Princeton man. A handsome, ivy-clad stone building with a classic clock tower, it lends itself well to a print. The next spring I made the sketch and wished that I were young enough to wear a white beer jacket the way the Princeton boys did. The Nassau Hall drypoint was approved, and I printed up the edition on my old French press, which was quite a chore. The work load was getting heavy, and my correspondence lagged. I thought longingly of the efficient Sergeant Krenz who had been such a help in Bushy Park, and finally located her in far-off Saskatchewan. She agreed to leave the farm and to come to our little New England seaport as my secretary. Life became much simpler with her arrival. She stayed sixteen years in the studio over the grocery store, and made it run like clockwork.

Being freed from details, I felt justified in succumbing to spring fever, especially since Virginia was beckoning. After protracted talks with my friends in Colonial Williamsburg, they had agreed to give their blessing to a proposed illustrated book to be called *Behold Wil-*

Kitchen of the Blair House, from *Behold Williamsburg*

liamsburg. They also volunteered to check my text for accuracy, to furnish interior views, and to appear on the title page. Thus stimulated, I bought a new Speed Graphic to supplement my Orix, and hurried to the ancient capitol of Virginia. It was radiant with fruit blossoms and dogwood, and the foliage was lacy—sheer paradise for the photographer. The weather was kind, and I scurried about with my tripod, camera, and black cloth as long as the sun held out. A good harvest of spring pictures was the result, but an autumn visit was also needed to complete the book. Drypoints, pencil drawings, and pen-and-ink end papers were added when the volume appeared in 1947. Much has happened in Williamsburg since then, but this book still serves as an acceptable "period piece."

Another opportunity soon arose in Virginia. The Mount Vernon Ladies Association of the Union wanted a new handbook of George Washington's home. They engaged Yale's eminent printer, Carl Purington Rollins, to design the book, and asked me to take the photographs, including color covers. This was one of the happiest of assignments, and we still cherish a close friendship with Charles C. Wall, the Resident Director of Mount Vernon, and his family.

The Williamsburg book had the pleasant aftereffect of bringing

The West Parlor, Mount Vernon, from *Mount Vernon, A Handbook*

137

The RCA Building from Madison Avenue,
from *Rockefeller Center, A
Photographic Narrative*

The Channel, from *Rockefeller Center,
A Photographic Narrative*

my name before Caroline Hood, the most attractive and dynamic director of Public Relations at Rockefeller Center. She is the niece of Raymond Hood, one of the original architects of this great landmark in New York, and she wanted a handbook for visitors. Kenneth Chorley, then president of Colonial Williamsburg, suggested that she talk to me, and she told her secretary to get me on the telephone. A number of calls came through, and my good wife explained that I was in my studio, where there was no phone. Would Miss Hood please call at dinner time? "What do you mean, he can't come to the phone? Get Mr. Chamberlain right away, or else!" was Miss Hood's exasperated reply to that.

It took two days to get us together on a line, and Miss Hood distinctly was not amused. Luckily I was due to come to New York anyway, and I entered her office with distinct trepidation. There were a few awkward moments, perhaps, but then we went out to a good French restaurant, had an apéritif and a resounding good bottle of Burgundy, and the whole problem was resolved in minutes. That's the nice thing about making books. You also make fast friends—for life. Outside her office hours Miss Hood is Mrs. John Carlin, and the Carlin-Chamberlain friendship has enjoyed two flourishing decades.

The handbook was called *Rockefeller Center, a Photographic Narrative,* and it involved writing and designing a pictorial document using the black-and-white work of many photographers. Today it appears largely in color, and is carried by many visitors who take the guided tour of Rockefeller Center.

Another close friendship developed in working with the sage of Beacon Hill, Mark Antony DeWolfe Howe. I had known this venerable all-round man of letters at the Tavern Club in Boston, and admired his rich, bell-like voice as he led the singing of the Christmas carols. Mark invited me to his house on Louisburg Square and discussed his newest project, the story of twelve famous landmarks in Boston. Fresh pictures were needed to show Faneuil Hall, the Old State House, the Old North Church, King's Chapel, the Public Garden and other historic treasures. The dear old man asked if I would take the pictures and design the book, an offer that was accepted with joy. I spent many Sundays in Boston with my camera, free from the vexation of traffic, and obtained most of the pictures Mr. Howe desired.

Boston Landmarks, published by Hastings House, was a quiet and attractive little book, but caused no perceptible sensation. Five years later we collaborated on another volume, *Who Lived Here?* This was "A Baker's Dozen of Historic New England Houses and Their Occupants," and brought in such diverse personalities as Louisa May Alcott, Anne Bradstreet, Emily Dickinson, John Brown of Providence, Paul Revere, and the Adamses of Quincy. There were thirteen houses to visit and photograph, inside and out. A trip to Nantucket brought the home of Maria Mitchell, the first woman astronomer in America, into focus. An expedition to South Berwick, Maine, revealed the house where Sarah Orne Jewett wrote *The Country of the Pointed Firs.* As a young man, Mark Howe had known Miss Jewett. *Who Lived Here* was a brilliant collection of essays, and when the book was published

Gore Place, Waltham, Massachusetts, from *Who Lived Here?*

by Little, Brown and Co., it was rewarded by fine reviews and sprightly sales. Modest royalties are still paid by the publisher, but it is a little disconcerting to receive the check, which is now made out to "The Estate of Samuel Chamberlain."

The publication of *Who Lived Here* seemed to me to call for a testimonial of some sort to the distinguished author. After waiting hopefully for some gesture from the publishers, I decided to give my own cocktail party for Mark Howe and his friends at the Club of Odd Volumes on Boston's Beacon Hill. It turned out to be a decided success, and Mark was wreathed in smiles. Several members of the publishing house accepted my invitation, and seemed faintly embarrassed. One of them took me by the arm and said "Well, this is the first time that I've seen the author of one of our books give a party for the publishers!"

There are numerous print clubs scattered over our country, and many of them follow the tradition of publishing a presentation print annually for their members. The great majority of our graphic artists have worked with the clubs by making a print especially for them. Before World War II, I made a drypoint for the Society of American Etchers, that gave a bird's-eye view of the marketplace in Senlis. Now in this first postwar year of 1946 came an offer from Mr. Ernest A.

Louisburg Square, Boston,
from *Boston Landmarks*

The Harbor Side, Friendship, Maine

Hospital Santa Cruz, Toledo

Melchert, President of the Chicago Society of Etchers, to make the yearly presentation plate. I submitted a pencil drawing of the most Yankee-flavored subject I knew, a lobsterman's shingled shack at the water's edge of a Maine seacoast village. Lobster pots cluttered the foreground, and the whole subject was a trifle unkempt. Mr. Melchert approved the drawing and the drypoint appeared as "The Harbor Side—Friendship, Maine" in December. The three hundred impressions were handsomely printed by Charles White in New York.

Without trying to put them in chronological order, I recall other presentation plates. One drypoint was made from an early pen-and-ink sketch of the Hospital Santa Cruz in Toledo, Spain, and went to the Rochester Print Club. A pencil sketch of a tall clock tower in Moulins, France, called Jacquemart, was translated into drypoint for the Rockford, Illinois, Print Club. Our enterprising little Marblehead Arts Association founded a print club of its own called "Friends of Contemporary Prints," and published, among several other plates, my drypoint called "Summer Shadows." It shows the old King Hooper Mansion, home of the association. Frank Benson, Arthur Heintzelman, Thomas Nason, Sam Thal, and several other American printmakers contributed to this thriving club in its heyday.

In addition to presentation prints, many an etcher is approached on

Early Morning Market, Senlis

Summer Shadows, Marblehead, The King Hooper Mansion

The Old Bubier Mansion, Marblehead

somewhat more commercial projects. It is natural for a bank president to want an etching of his own soaring skyscraper, and since etchers have families to feed, like everybody else, they usually grasp at such a commission. I have made drypoints of three banks, one each in New York, Boston, and Chicago, and once in a while I wonder just how many windows they represent. Smaller etching opportunities also arise, and at one time the label on Lydia Pinkham's consoling tonic for pale people was reproduced from two etchings. Arthur Heintzelman made the portrait of Lydia, and I etched the ornamental border!

Late in 1946 a persistent dream came true, and we were able to buy the old Bubier mansion in Marblehead, a venerable gambrel-roofed house with a huge central brick chimney. It was built on a solid dome of rock on the steep end of Tucker Street, and according to the records available, probably dates from 1698. At one time it was used by the town to house elderly people, and later was subdivided into four, and then two apartments. It is a fascinating old place with six fireplaces built into the central chimney. Most of the rooms have good eight-

Jacquemart, the town belfry in Moulins, France (drypoint)

Jacquemart (original pencil drawing)

eenth-century paneling and wide pine floorboards. It was shy on bath-rooms and heating, and underwent a basic restoration before we were able to take possession. It remains a joy to us today, and we are convinced that there is nothing more satisfying than an old New England house.

The next spring, following the usual execrable New England winter, a new era of photographic projects dawned. My faithful Orix camera had become obsolete, since nobody in America any longer made film to fit it. To supplant it, I found a used 5 x 7-inch Linhof view camera with three lenses and a fine rising front. This opened up new horizons. Composing a picture on the larger ground glass of this camera was an adventure. High-speed, fine-grain cut film was available, and best of all, sheets of 5 x 7 color film could be used. By assembling a color subject carefully on the ground glass, it was possible to obtain a rich watercolor subject, not in a few hours, but in 1/25th of a second. That really shattered me, and color sheet film has been a part of the budget ever since.

Three books were on the back of the stove that summer. One was a revised edition of *Open House in New England,* an illustrated, cap-

Doorway of the Harvard Club, Boston

143

Harvard Yard and Memorial Church in Midwinter, from *Fair Harvard*

Parson Capen House, 1783, Topsfield, Massachusetts, from *Open House in New England*

tioned guide to historic houses that were open to the public. This had first been published in 1937 by the Stephen Daye Press, in Brattleboro, Vermont. Hastings House took over the subsequent printings.

Donald Moffat, a loyal and eloquent son of Harvard, suggested that we combine forces to make a pictorial record of his Alma Mater. The Harvard University Press was hospitable to the idea, and I was furnished with a cherished special pass that permitted me to take photographs with a tripod in the Harvard yard. The Harvard police had to respect it. The photographic task spread through the following fall and winter. Don Moffat wrote a long, affectionate and inspired foreword, an essay on Harvard that has been reprinted on countless occasions. *Fair Harvard* appeared in 1948, and went straight to the heart of Harvard men.

Six New England Villages was something quite different, a study of life in rural America as exemplified in six Yankee communities. In purely arbitrary fashion, I selected a particularly attractive village in each of the six New England states—Hancock, New Hampshire, Litchfield, Connecticut, Little Compton, Rhode Island, Old Benning-

144

Mount Anthony, Old Bennington, Vermont   The Amasa Gray House, 1684, Little Compton, Rhode Island

From *Six New England Villages*

ton, Vermont, Old Deerfield, Massachusetts, and Wiscasset, Maine. Eighteen pages of gravure were devoted to each, and the contrast between them is striking.

This year of 1947 wasn't all devoted to gadding about with a camera. At one point I flew to Grand Rapids, where the American Institute of Architects was having its annual convention. There they awarded me their Fine Arts Gold Medal for "Distinguished Achievement in Etching."

A detailed account of my New England books that ensued over the next few years would make dull reading. There was a minor torrent of them, but they seemed to fit a touristic demand. Our constant aim was to provide well-illustrated, inexpensive books for visitors, similar to those they would find in their travels abroad. Any number of subjects were approached with this object in view. *Princeton in Spring* was a happy aftermath of Elmer Adler's hospitality in inviting me to visit his print center just after the war. The Princeton University Press suggested a book that relied entirely on photographs, with the simplest titles and a one-page foreword. Blessed with idyllic weather four days out of five, I was able to take pictures of the University and Princeton's historic houses framed in the first suspicion of April foliage and the full splendor of May blossoms.

The Derelicts, Wiscasset, Maine,
from *Six New England Villages*

145

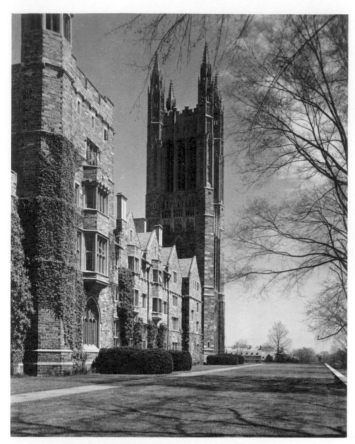

Cleveland Tower, Graduate College, Princeton

From *Princeton in Spring*

The White Church, Princeton

Courtyard of Pierson College, Yale,
from *The Yale Scene*

After Harvard and Princeton, it was only natural to turn to New Haven, where my friends at the Yale University Press wanted an illustrated book to be published on the occasion of Yale's two hundred and fiftieth anniversary. They not only provided me with a pass to photograph on the campus, but they hired a student to carry my paraphernalia and engaged a group of well-dressed undergraduates (with polished shoes) to lend human interest to my pictures. This was luxury indeed. The book showed Yale in all seasons of the year, and methodically covered the different colleges, some "Colonial" in style, others conceived in James Gamble Rogers late collegiate Gothic. English Professor Robert D. French, the greatly loved master of Jonathan Edwards College, wrote an eloquent introduction to *The Yale Scene,* and composed the captions as well. The book appeared in 1950 and is something of a "period piece" also, coming before the wave of modern architecture that has transformed, and doubtless improved, the Yale image. There are intimate views of Mory's and the straw-hatted boys and gals having fun on Derby Day; most of the book dwells on Yale's handsome buildings.

Salem Interiors was a winter project. Using floodlights extensively for the first time, my industrious wife and I acted as a team. She tended the floodlights and I handled the camera. We photographed the venerable houses of neighboring Salem from the House of Seven Gables (1668) to the nineteenth-century mansions of clipper ship captains on Chestnut Street. The masterful wood carving of Samuel Mc-

146

Court of Branford College in Springtime, from *The Yale Scene*

Bedroom in the Richard Derby House, 1760

From *Salem Interiors*

Rear Parlor of the Pingree House, 1804

The Bishop Huntington House,
from *Forty Acres*

Intire furnished some of the finest details. *Forty Acres* concerned the beautiful Bishop Huntington house in Hadley, Massachusetts. Dr. James Lincoln Huntington, a dear man who has ushered thousands of babies into this world, wrote the text and asked me to make the photographic illustrations.

New England has developed a few historic communities for visitors from all over our own country and abroad, and they have met with an enthusiastic reception. Old Sturbridge Village, near Worcester, Massachusetts, gives an accurate impression of an industrious inland neighborhood as it looked in the early 1800's. Old buildings have been assembled around a village green, and the visiting public sees the early arts and crafts demonstrated by talented artisans. Mystic Seaport is something quite different, a restored shipbuilding town near the mouth of the Mystic River in southern Connecticut. Here are moored a few famous ships, including the *Charles W. Morgan,* last of the great whaling vessels, the training ship *Joseph Conrad* and the *Bowdoin,* Admiral MacMillan's staunch vessel that sailed for nearly forty years in Arctic waters. There is a cobblestone seaport street, with a counting house, general store, tavern, schoolhouse, clock shop and a marine ironworker's plant. Of course there is a rope walk, a yacht club building and a museum, and they fascinate the visitors, especially the

The *Charles W. Morgan,* last of the great whaling vessels, from *Mystic Seaport*

Miner Grant's General Store in Midwinter, from *A Tour of Old Sturbridge Village*

The Old Covered Bridge,
from *A Tour of Old Sturbridge Village*

children. Both of these living communities requested illustrated handbooks, which need frequent revision. Public response to both communities has been almost phenomenal, and so many changes and improvements have been made that it is hard to keep up with them. I still make periodic trips, using both color and black-and-white film for new editions of the handbooks.

Old Deerfield is a mile-long village in Western Massachusetts that was the scene of a tragic invasion by the Indians in the early eighteenth century. The Deerfield massacre is known to every schoolboy. Today not a trace of violence remains. The serene elm-grown settlement is the picture of tranquillity. Deerfield Academy is here, and in addition there is a procession of fine old New England houses, about a dozen of which are furnished with antiques and open to the public. Most of them are the property of the Heritage Foundation, and are restored due to the devotion and enthusiasm of Mr. and Mrs. Henry N. Flynt. Here indeed is a perfect subject for a book, and I worked with Mr. Flynt in preparing one called *Frontier of Freedom,* "The Soul and Substance of America Portrayed in One Extraordinary Village." So many changes took place that we made up a completely new book in 1965 entitled *Historic Deerfield, Houses and Interiors.*

The Frary House, 1683, Deerfield, Massachusetts
From *Historic Deerfield, Houses and Interiors*

Fireplace in the Ballroom of the Hall Tavern

At Eastern Point in Gloucester, Massachusetts, a gifted decorator and architect named Henry Sleeper built a most extraordinary house of twenty-six rooms, each in a different architectural style, and each furnished with authentic pieces of the corresponding period. It was named "Beauport," and well deserved to be called "The Most Fascinating House in America." Paul Hollister wrote the text and captions for *Beauport,* and I made most of the photographs under rather unusual circumstances—in the middle of winter. The house was a summer residence only, and had no heating plant whatsoever. The temperature on the day appointed for photography was fourteen degrees above zero, but in the house itself it was only eight above. The custodian, a burly native of Gloucester named George Wanson, unlocked the front door and quickly built a wood fire in the massive fireplace of the Jacobean Room. Meanwhile I went about the frigid business of making time exposures of the interiors with floodlights. They offered scant warmth, but I was equipped with multiple sweaters and scarves, a Cossack's headpiece and earmuffs to combat the cold. Mr. Wanson sat by his fire and had a hot toddy ready for me whenever numbness set in. The job was finished in two days, and all of the pictures had the warmth of a June morning.

The Jacobean Room, from *Beauport*

151

Chez l'Ami Jean, Bourg-en-Bresse, from *Bouquet de France*

Louhans, from *Bouquet de France*

Before we knew it, three years and more had scurried merrily along in the pursuit of the American Scene. But in the background lay a dormant nostalgia for Europe, particularly France. We had no urge to return to our battered house in Senlis, but to travel over France once again in a small car was something else. The yearning for another "Traveling Fellowship" was becoming acute. News dispatches indicated that bridges in France had been rebuilt, roads were once again in good shape and, best of all, that rationing was practically terminated and French gastronomy was assuming its old splendor.

Earle MacAusland, the publisher of *Gourmet,* thought it would be a good idea to initiate a new series of illustrated articles on French food, wine and travel in his magazine. His proposal met with a positive and excited response from the senior Chamberlains. Our first move, after applying for passports, was to acquire a new French automobile to be delivered in Paris. If we had been French, we would have had to remain for years on a waiting list, but since we were paying in badly needed American dollars, the purchase of a car on a "Transit Temporaire" basis with TT license plates was possible. The red tape was rather ponderous, but finally the transaction was completed

The Chateau de Villebon, from *Bouquet de France*

through the New York representatives of Peugeot, the famous French firm that manufactures anything from pepper mills to locomotives.

In the meantime, a pleasant little ceremony in the French Consulate in Boston had further cemented our affection for *la belle France*. In February, 1949, the Consul General, Monsieur Chambon, pinned the cross of Chevalier de la Légion d'Honneur on my lapel, accompanied by the customary buss on each cheek. We toasted our projected French gastronomic foray with the good Moët et Chandon champagne that followed the ceremony.

Early that spring the two of us crossed the Atlantic on an old favorite, the *De Grasse*. This sturdy ship had undergone the indignity of being sunk by the Germans in the Gironde River, but had been refloated and refurbished, and reigned for the moment as the flagship of the French Line transatlantic fleet. And how does one build up prestige in such a situation? By serving superlative food, of course. The cuisine of the unostentatious *De Grasse* was at that moment more succulent, meticulous and luxurious than that of any ship plying the Atlantic. And the service was immaculate. I doubt if even today's *France* serves better food. After a memorable voyage we were once again in Paris, staying in our favorite Left Bank Hotel des Saints-Pères, taking a ceremonial Vermouth Cassis at the Café des Deux Magots, and indulging in *choucroute garnie* at the famous Brasserie Lipp. Our coveted Peugeot 203 was waiting in a garage, and appeared

Burgundy Village, from *Bouquet de France*

153

Abbaye de Montmajour, near Arles, from *Bouquet de France*

Porte St. Jacques, Parthenay,
from *Bouquet de France*

infinitely desirable. Furthermore it was protected with elaborate locking devices to thwart the car thieves who were very active at the time. Motoring in Paris was a joy. The streets were open and one could park almost anywhere. Traffic jams that plague Paris today were unknown then.

But we were impatient to get to the country and begin the extended "Epicurean Tour of the French Provinces" that was to appear in *Gourmet*. Without realizing it at the time, this was a turning point in our careers. The noble art of gastronomy was creeping in, and the graphic arts were beginning to serve as accomplices to the epicurean theme. In the rear trunk of the little Peugeot were two cameras, a small Super-Ikonta BX and the large 5 x 7 Linhof that had served so well in previous years. There were many fat boxes of unexposed cut film, a dozen film holders, a tripod and a black changing bag that served as a portable dark room. Needless to say, there was an ample supply of sketch pads, watercolor blocks and hot pressed paper for pen and ink. We were all set for the great adventure.

Our advance planning had been thorough, and we were well fortified with road maps and careful notes on the hotels, restaurants and historic sites to be visited. With all of France to choose from, where

154

Valley of the Var, from *Bouquet de France*

should this epicurean tour begin? We did not hesitate a moment, and headed our new Peugeot straight for the small province of La Bresse, adjoining Burgundy. This was a fountainhead of fine provincial cooking, and the home of the greatest gastronome of them all, Jean Anthèlme Brillat-Savarin. We stayed in the great man's home town of Belley, visited his birthplace, and put up there for the night at the venerable Hôtel Pernollet. For dinner we were regaled with an incomparable *feuilleté aux queues d'écrevisse* with a crisp white wine of the region, Roussette de Virieu. This was followed by a regal *poulet à la Reine* accompanied by a Chambertin 1934, and we decided that this indeed was a savory way to practice journalism. Later in the evening we became acquainted with young Monsieur Pernollet, a fourth-generation member of this hotel family, and asked him for a few historical notes and some favorite recipes. He complied with a smile and gave us a few menus and his *carte des vins* as well. We left the next morning

Regional map, from *Bouquet de France*

155

Ostellerie du Vieux Pérouges

From *Bouquet de France*

Low Tide at Le Tréport, Normandy

The Dunce-cap House, Kaysersberg,
from *Bouquet de France*

with the pertinent facts of the hotel and the touristic virtues of the town duly inscribed in a notebook.

This first hotel visit is described in some detail because it is typical of scores of interviews that ensued during the next few months. Before our Bressan adventure was over we stayed in Bourg-en-Bresse and learned the true story of the famous *poulardes de Bresse* that are considered the finest roasting fowl in the world. We stopped at the Hôtel de France in Nantua and learned from Monsieur Pauchard, the owner-chef, the secret of *Sauce Nantua,* one of the world's great sauces for fish. In Pérouges, an historic and almost unblemished medieval hill town, we went to the ancient timbered Ostellerie du Vieux Pérouges and dined on *fonds d'artichauts Lucullus, morilles à la creme,* and the authentic *poularde de Bresse* roasted on the spit before a wood fire, accompanied by an old Richebourg.

In Priay, a tiny hamlet, we lunched at the Hôtel Bourgeois. This was a simple country inn, but there is a story behind it. Back in 1926 we had dined at this hotel and had met Madame Marie Bourgeois, the demure little woman who presided in the kitchen. The menu that she provided was truly extraordinary, and we found out that she had been adjudged the best cook in France not once but *twice*. At the *Concours Gastronomique et Culinaire* in Paris she was awarded this honor, and was chosen to prepare the official dinner for the Président de la République and his distinguished guests at the Grand Palais. After the dinner when she appeared for the grand ovation, she was kissed on

156

Semur-en-Auxois in Burgundy, from *Bouquet de France*

Chateau Farm, Saint Magnance, from *Bouquet de France*

Farm Gate at Balagny

both cheeks by a corn-fed Minister of Agriculture and given a testimonial parchment. Then she quietly returned to Priay. When we arrived this time, the famed parchment was still on the wall, but Madame Bourgeois, alas, was no more. The last visit in La Bresse took us to the Hôtel du Chapon Fin, in the little town of Thoissey. This is the citadel of Monsieur Paul Blanc, today considered one of the ten foremost chefs in France. Here we encountered *escargots de Bourgogne, quenelles de Brochet Nantua,* and *chapon à la crème* in a Lucullan dinner that justified Monsieur Blanc's lofty reputation. This summed up the highlights of the first gastronomic province.

Here, as in other provincial hotels, we became acquainted with the chef and asked to taste his culinary specialties and one of his recommended wines. We did not disclose our journalistic mission, and always paid our bill. Sometimes we joined our host for an after-dinner brandy or a friendly bottle of champagne, but the taint of commercialism never marred the picture.

The first chapter of the epicurean tours of the French provinces appeared in *Gourmet* embellished by a good deal of calligraphy and a few vignettes. There was a small map of La Bresse, pointing out the shrines of gastronomic interest, also an etching of the countryside and a pencil drawing of a venerable Bressan restaurant. Impressive indeed were the recipes, translated and adapted by my completely bilingual wife. The famous *Fondue de Belley,* lobster butter, and an utterly divine preparation called *Gateau de Foies Blonds de Poularde de Bresse Baigné de la Sauce aux Queues d'Ecrevisses* were translated into simple basic kitchen English.

158

Manoir de Mémorin, Lusigny, from *Bouquet de France*

The same textual pattern was applied to each succeeding province—first a résumé of the gastronomic virtues, a word on its wine, restaurants and hotels, a personality or two, a pleasant handful of recipes, a map and a few drawings. Our energetic little Peugeot (which had a few bugs, I must admit) carried us through Burgundy where we formed a lasting friendship with Alexandre Dumaine, one of the most inspired masters of *la grande cuisine,* and his charming, English-speaking wife. I sketched the ancient wine press in the Clos de Vougeot and the picturesque streets of Beaune. We visited the famous Foire Gastronomique in Dijon, as I had done decades before in the Senlis days. In Vienne, on the banks of the Rhone, we dined at the Restaurant de la Pyramide, the topmost shrine of gastronomy anywhere, and interviewed the famous Fernand Point and his wife and successor, Mado.

The summer passed all too quickly as we wandered over Alsace, Savoy, the Nivernais, and Provence. The photographic opportunities were endless, and the faithful Linhof worked overtime. The only drawback was that this camera used cut film in holders, and I had only twelve of them, each holding two films. Once the twenty-four films were exposed, it was necessary to resort to the changing bag, an ingenious contraption that permits the photographer to change supersensitive film in broad daylight. Without going into details, it is possible to put a box of unexposed film and the twelve film holders in this black bag, and by feel and patient manipulation unload the exposed film and recharge the holders with a fresh supply. But to do this, a fairly large table is needed. Some hotel rooms have them, but many do not. I have found myself changing film on a billiard table or in a

The author with Alexandre Dumaine, one of the greatest of French chefs, at the Hotel de la Côte-d'Or in Saulieu

Market Day, Auxerre, from *Bouquet de France*

From *Bouquet
de France*

hotel dining room after hours, or even in a French café at apéritif time. There I would sit with my arms in this mysterious black bag, manipulating film, while the passing public stared in total perplexity. It's one of the hazards of photography, and one becomes hardened to it.

One season was only the beginning of this epicurean pilgrimage. Covering all of France, Paris included, was a task that took time. We were back again in the summers of 1950 and 1951 with cameras, sketchpads, notebooks and tastebuds. A new set of tires was needed for the Peugeot, and there was a certain pressure on the waistline. Each of our daughters joined us for a time. Narcisse was working in the Paris office of *Newsweek,* and Stephanie came over for a vacation.

We revisited the Riviera and pried into the secret of *bouillabaisse.* In Languedoc we saw Carcassonne, Albi and the Pont du Gard, and learned how to make the genuine *cassoulet de Castelnaudery.* Across the Pyrenees our path led to the Basque country and the authentic formula for *piperade,* the famous Basque egg dish. In Bordeaux we visited the vineyards and the cellars, and dined at the Chapon Fin, then the greatest restaurant in southwestern France. In Périgord we visited a truffle expert, and watched geese being stuffed with grain so that their livers would yield that supreme delicacy, *paté de foie gras.* The path led northward through the Cognac country which is also

160

The Ancient Wine Press, Clos de Vougeot, from *Bouquet de France*

blessed with superb Romanesque churches, and on to the Loire valley, famed for its châteaux, then Brittany, Normandy, and finally Paris.

Every month *Gourmet* printed an illustrated chapter of our epicurean tour, and the reaction of their readers was favorable. Certainly the letters that we received were encouraging. The way seemed clear to make a definitive volume out of so much material, and there was no epicurean pilgrimage in 1952. Instead I stayed in Marblehead editing and rewriting the articles, and sending out letters with questionnaires to the hundreds of hotels and restaurants that we had visited. In addition to routine questions about ownership, specialties of the house, and such things, we asked for additional regional recipes. The response was terrific, and hundreds of tempting recipes rolled in. Some were purposely vague, but most of them were filled with priceless information. By using these and consulting our own extensive library of French cookbooks, my resourceful wife kitchen-tested and assembled a superb collection of regional recipes translated into basic culinary English.

Truffle Hunters,
from *Bouquet de France*

The *Gourmet* people gave me complete freedom in designing the new book which bore the title of *Bouquet de France* (my wife's in-

161

Lobsterman's Shack, Rockport   Timeworn Shore, Annisquam

From *Cape Ann Through the Seasons*

The Blue Atlantic, Orleans Beach,
from *Cape Cod*

spiration). I laid out each of the chapters with pen and pencil sketches and photographic illustrations, maps, marginal vignettes and tailpieces. The name of each recommended restaurant or hotel was shown in the margin in calligraphy. Looking back at it, I am aghast at the amount of work involved. The letterpress part of the book and the binding were done by the Kingsport Press, Inc., in Kingsport, Tennessee. Sheet-fed gravure was used to reproduce the drawings and photographs, and this was done by the Beck Engraving Co. in Philadelphia. Combining the two elements of the book was a problem for the binder, who succeeded admirably. Complete with Earle MacAusland's introduction, my foreword, my wife's treasury of French recipes, and thirty chapters on regional food and travel with copious illustrations, *Bouquet de France* was published in November, 1952, and subsequently went through seven printings. Hamish Hamilton distributed it in London with encouraging results.

It was time for a shift of scenery from Europe, and I spent much of the next year making forays into Cape Ann, Cape Cod, Nantucket, and the Berkshires with a brand new Linhof camera with a fine widefield Ektar lens. My objective was to obtain a photographic impression of each area so that visitors could acquire an attractive illustrated volume at a reasonable cost. Captions were cut to a minimum, but the pictures were taken under perfect conditions of sun and shadow. This required a great deal of patience, and once in a while I wonder how

162

Elihu Coleman House, 1722, Nantucket

Wharf Rats Club, Nantucket

From *Nantucket, A Photographic Sketchbook*

Pole Wharf, Provincetown, from *Cape Cod*

Lobster Pot Panorama, Chatham, from *Cape Cod*

The Village Green in Autumn, Alford

Fawn Lake in Midsummer, Sheffield

From *The Berkshires, A Camera Impression*

Château de Chenonceaux,
from *Soft Skies of France*

much of my life has been spent in disconsolately standing beside my camera waiting for the sun to come out from behind a cloud. Patience had its reward, and four pictorial books, printed in gravure, were the result of the year's work.

In addition, a nostalgic volume called *Soft Skies of France* appeared in 1953. I have always contended that the skies that hover over France have a limpid quality found nowhere else, and this collection of a hundred and forty full-page pictures set out to prove it. Artistically it was a joy, but its sales performance was languid.

Hastings House has continued its sponsorship of our books, publishing an average of one a year. *Old Rooms for New Living* was a treatise on early New England houses from the early American period to post-Federal times. My able wife, who knows as much about interior decoration as she does about cooking, wrote this book, using my photographs of New England interiors. It has chapters on halls and stairways, living rooms and libraries, dining rooms and kitchens, bedrooms, fireplaces and window treatments. Altogether it makes an informative handbook for the home builder.

An opportunity to escape the harsh rigors of a New England winter arose when the Charleston Historical Foundation invited us to come to that hospitable city in South Carolina and make a book on the interiors of its historic houses. This was too good to miss. We had seen several books on Charleston and had a fair idea of the fine paneling,

164

Spring Morning, Lac d'Annecy, from *Soft Skies of France*

The Hills above Barcellonette, front endpaper of *Soft Skies of France*

Blockfront Secretary, Ashley House, Deerfield   Samuel McIntire Carving, Pingree House, Salem

From *Old Rooms for New Living*

Hallway of the Mission House, Stockbridge,
from *Old Rooms for New Living*

wood carving and period furniture that graced its dignified mansions. Mrs. Frances Edmunds, the secretary of the foundation, found us an apartment with a garden and arranged to have us interviewed and photographed by the Charleston *News and Courier*. The story appeared on the society page, telling of our hope that Charlestonians would help us in our attempt to make a beautiful book of interiors. That did it. The telephone began to jingle the next day. Not a single home owner refused to allow us to take interior views. We've never met more charming or more coöperative people. "Come around any day at Bourbon time" was the cordial greeting we heard on every side. It took two eventful winters to cover the subject photographically, and to write the text. It was hard work, too, poking under sofas for base plugs, holding floodlights aloft, and focusing the camera on one's knees. We worked steadily and on a few occasions even photographed two houses a day. *Southern Interiors of Charleston, South Carolina,* was an ambitious book of 172 pages, large in format, warm in tone, and expensive. Our daughter Narcisse edited the text, and Hastings House published it. When the book appeared in 1956 the Charlestonians seemed to be pleased. We long to return there some winter without having to grope for base plugs.

A group of eminent New Yorkers who have not forgotten their New England ancestry long ago founded the New England Society in the City of New York. Their One Hundred and Fiftieth Anniversary

Mantel of the Branford-Horry House, from *Southern Interiors of Charleston, South Carolina*

Drawing Room of the Colonel John Stuart House   The Green Drawing Room, Nathaniel Russell House
From *Southern Interiors of Charleston, South Carolina*

Chandelier in the Manigault House,
Charleston, from *Southern Interiors*

Dinner was held at the Plaza in December, 1955, and, as is its custom, the Society made a literary award. This was one of the rare occasions when I have found myself at the speaker's table. I was seated between Governor Christian Herter of Massachusetts, and Reginald Townsend, to whom I once sold pencil drawings when he was an art editor. There were Blue Point oysters, New England clam chowder, Vermont turkey and pumpkin pie, and at the conclusion came the toasts. Reggie Townsend then made a pleasant speech and gave me the award, a handsome desk clock, "for all that I had done for New England." There was polite applause from the guests and the New England governors present, as I took my place at the lectern for a brief acknowledgment. At least, I meant it to be brief, but my soporific effect must have been immediate, and deadly. Midway between the first two sentences a news photographer caught the scene at the head table, and it showed Governor Herter and Governor Dennis Roberts of Rhode Island both in deep slumber, while Governor Johnson of Vermont gazed dreamily at the ceiling. It might have been the photographer's flash, but I keep this picture handy as a reminder that public speaking is not my particular cup of tea.

The success of the French provincial articles and of *Bouquet de France* encouraged us to carry on further epicurean research, this time in Italy. We were traveling in Southern France with Stephanie in the summer of 1953, and made a reconnaissance trip to the Italian

Via Appia Antica, Rome, from *Italian Bouquet*

Riviera. Far less sophisticated than its French counterpart, this bright crescent of shore facing the Mediterranean is verdant, unpretentious and hospitable. There are enough sketchable towns such as Camogli and Portofino to make it a joy to artists, and there are culinary specialties such as *trenette al pesto* and *cima di vitello* to bring felicity to the epicure. Here was abundant material for the first installment of "A Gastronomic Tour of Italy." Armed with a carefully compiled notebook, we dined at a variety of good places from the palatial Royal Hotel in San Remo down to the little family Trattoria Rina in Genoa. The weather was warm, and there was a chance to make a few pencil drawings.

When it came time to make up the first article for *Gourmet* we settled in the friendly Hotel Savoia-Beeler in Nervi, just east of Genoa. It was owned and managed by a Swiss family, and had been a strong favorite with the top military brass during the war. If Marshall Kesselring's signature is on one page of the guest book, General Mark Clark's is on the next! In a sunbathed room overlooking the sea it was pleasant to type out my manuscript on a portable Smith Corona and to make the illustrations which included a headpiece drawing, hand-lettered title and calligraphic subtitle, a map of the region and a few vignettes. In the autumn my wife sailed back to America to be with her mother in California, and during the following winter I traveled alone in Italy. My studio was a room in a hotel or *pensione,* sometimes cheerful,

Mattarana, from *Italian Bouquet*

169

Perugia, from *Italian Bouquet*

The Harbor, Camogli, from *Italian Bouquet*

but often a bit melancholy. Italy has its gloomy winters too, and there was scant cheer for the outdoor artist.

The linguistic problem was less difficult, but far from perfect. I had studied Italian, and had picked up a good deal during World War II. This permitted me to read the newspapers and magazines with ease, and to understand most conversations when they weren't loaded with slang. But I spoke Italian with a certain hesitation and lack of confidence, and I have always kicked myself that I didn't settle down and really learn to speak it with total fluency. Still this didn't prevent me from ordering a good meal, making friends with the maître d'hôtel and the wine waiter, and obtaining some savory Italian recipes from the chef.

My base in Florence was the charming Pensione Consigli, and it took more than a month to cover Tuscany and its shrines of good cooking. During this time I received a request from Alice Winchester, editor of *Antiques,* to prepare an illustrated article on I Tatti, the hillside villa on the outskirts of Florence that had been for years the home of the famous Bernard Berenson. The old gentleman was most cordial, invited me to lunch twice, and allowed me to take all the interior pictures I wanted, provided I used no floodlights or flash. I also photographed "B. B.", then in his late eighties, on his morning walk through his garden with Signorina Nicky Mariano, his secretary. This picture appears as the frontispiece in Miss Mariano's recent memoirs of the great critic, collector and bibliophile.

Bernard Berenson with Nicky Mariano
at I Tatti

171

Château de Fenis in the Valle d'Aosta, from *Italian Bouquet*

The Town Hall, Orta, from *Italian Bouquet*

Florence made up for its bad weather by a plenitude of good restaurants, some of them swank and pretentious, others simple *trattorie* that specialized in rapidly grilled Tuscan steaks and hearty flagons of Chianti. Side trips to Siena, Lucca, Pisa, and San Gimignano completed the gastronomic circuit of Tuscany, and I motored to Naples, hoping to find a spot of good weather there or on the Amalfi Drive. Instead the rain continued relentlessly, and I visited the few good Neapolitan restaurants in a mackintosh and rubbers. Amalfi, Ravello, Positano, Sorrento and Capri all had beckoning hotels, but the deluge cast a pall over them, and I found it difficult to write sprightly paragraphs.

Only when I crossed the straits of Messina and began a perimetal tour of Sicily did the weather clear. This is a marvelous way to spend a few leisurely weeks, and the little Peugeot rolled along into Palermo, and then to the glorious Greek temples at Segeste, Selinunte and Agrigento. A few sunny days in Siracusa, and I was back in Taormina, pounding my typewriter in a room at the Hôtel Metropole, where we had stayed during the Christmas season just thirty years before.

Early spring in Rome was a joyful sight. The sunshine was unfailing, and my camera worked overtime. It was warm enough to make pen-and-ink drawings along the Tiber and on the Via Appia. The great restaurants—Passetto, Alfredo, Ranieri, George's, and others—abounded in luxurious dishes, and the *salumerie,* the food shops, bulged with good things—hams, sausages, cheese, olives and wine. I

Church of San Stefano

VERONA

Church of San Stefano, Verona, from *Italian Bouquet*

Ponte Vecchio, Florence, from *Italian Bouquet*

Church of San Giovanni di Prè, Genoa,
from *Italian Bouquet*

couldn't help contrasting this portrait of plenty with Rome on its day of liberation in June, 1944. There just wasn't any food, or any electric power, and water could only be obtained at a trickle from street hydrants. This time my task was to cut food to a minimum, on doctor's orders, and still visit some thirty restaurants and order their specialties. A gastronomic reporter has his problems! Rome was noisy, and to obtain a spell of tranquillity I sometimes motored to Tivoli, Frascati and Viterbo to test dining places there.

The Roman holiday lasted about a month, and was followed by a tour of Umbria—Orvieto, Assisi, and Perugia, all cities of great beauty. The flat valley of the Po was next. Spread along the busy Via Emilia were a few noble cities—Piacenza, Parma, Modena and Bologna, each with photogenic cathedrals and worthy shrines of rich Bolognese cooking. In Ravenna I obtained permission to photograph the sublime mosaics inside the Church of San Vitale, and the results were thrilling.

The rich province of Veneto lay ahead, and after sketching, photographing and tasting in Verona, Vicenza and Padua, I drove the Peugeot into the enormous garage outside of Venice and took a gondola to my favorite *pensione*. The weather was perfect for photography, and I lugged my heavy Linhof camera, tripod and film case over countless bridges and endless embankments during the next

174

Broom Shop, Lucca, from *Italian Bouquet*

weeks. A treasury of sunny pictures was the result, about fifty times as many as I could use.

My good wife joined me on the next trip and during the summer of 1955 we explored Lombardy, Piedmont and the Dolomites in the north, the Adriatic coast, and the sunbaked southern provinces as well. Even with all this crisscrossing of Italy, our task was not finished, and it was necessary to return in the summer of 1956 to complete the gastronomic tour.

The Italian articles began in April, 1954, and ran intermittently in *Gourmet* over a period of three years. During much of 1957 I was busy rewriting them and preparing the dummy for the new book. Questionnaires had been sent to hundreds of restaurants in Italy, resulting in the usual rich harvest of culinary information. Invaluable assistance and encouragement came from Mrs. Manolita T. Doelger, director of the Italian State Tourist Office in New York, whose staff helped us with many of the intricacies of the Italian language. My wife prepared a seventy-five-page "Treasury of Italian Recipes" to bring our new book to a climax. It was called *Italian Bouquet* and contained eighteen regional chapters, all of them richly illustrated with drawings, maps and photographs. It was printed in the duotone offset process by Egmont H. Petersen, the celebrated Danish printer in Copenhagen. This process lends unusual richness to the photographic reproductions, and

Bordighera, from *Italian Bouquet*

175

Tower of the Church of Santa Maria in Cosmedin, Rome, from *Italian Bouquet*

Interior of the Church of San Vitale, Ravenna

Positano, from *Italian Bouquet*

greatly simplifies the layout problem as well. *Italian Bouquet,* bound in white as was its predecessor, was published in 1958, and we have all been happy about the reception it received. As a pleasurable postscript, the Italian Government awarded me the Stella Della Solidarità Italiana at a banquet gathering of Italophiles in New York.

Exhibitions in art galleries, museums and women's clubs are a part of every printmaker's life. They don't make very exciting reading, though, and I have made no attempt to list the private shows, lectures and print demonstrations that I have given throughout the years. A few occasions are vividly etched on my mind, however. One was a demonstration of making a drypoint on copper and printing it before the august Club of Odd Volumes in Boston. This was one of the few times I had stage fright. Seated in the front row only two feet away was Harvard's famed Professor George Lyman Kittredge, with his light grey salt-and-pepper suit and flowing white beard. He watched me like a hawk as I worked, and asked many questions, all of them very much to the point. I presented him with the first proof pulled from the drypoint, and hoped that I had not betrayed my nervousness.

One exhibition took place in Cambridge in February, 1956, that deserves particular mention. In the Charles Hayden Memorial Gallery at MIT an exhibition of eighty prints by four etchers was arranged. The four were George C. Wales, John Taylor Arms, Louis C. Rosen-

Regional map, from *Italian Bouquet*

177

Mont St. Michel, from the Embankment

The Crypt of Aquilon, Mont St. Michel

From *Mont St. Michel and Chartres*

South Aisle of Chartres Cathedral,
from *Mont St. Michel and Chartres*

berg, and Samuel Chamberlain, and all of them had studied architecture at the Institute. Twenty of the best prints by each etcher were hung in the handsome gallery. Mr. Wales's etchings all concerned sailing vessels, but the other three remained faithful to architectural subjects. There was an overtone of sadness to this exhibition, for Mr. Wales had left this world some fifteen years before, and the universally beloved John Taylor Arms had died at the age of sixty-six about two years previously.

Unforgettable also was the exhibition of my etchings, lithographs and drawings held in the Boston Public Library in May and June, 1961. Arthur Heintzelman, then Keeper of Prints at the Wiggin Collection, had arranged for the purchase of a generous assortment of my work in 1960. Beautifully matted and hung, the show was well reviewed and attended. This is a forerunner of my present happy relations with the Library, and I have always been grateful to Arthur, a long-time neighbor and friend, and one of the great American masters of etching.

Two new books, quite dissimilar, appeared about this time. One came from our kitchen, and was called *The Omelette Book,* by Narcissa G. Chamberlain. Alfred A. Knopf published this attractive volume, which was illustrated by Hilary Knight. It contained tested recipes for more than three hundred omelettes, and is just about the final word on the subject. Special English and German editions have

Romanesque Façade, Thaon, Normandy, from *Mont St. Michel and Chartres*

since been printed. Journalists and photographers descended upon my startled wife, asking her to demonstrate the technique of making a perfect omelette. A full-page color picture showing her with an omelette pan about to flip out its treasure appeared in *Sports Illustrated,* of all magazines.

The other volume was merely illustrated by my photographs. This was the Limited Editions Club printing of *Mont St. Michel and Chartres* by Henry Adams. I had admired this remarkable book ever since it had been required reading back in Technology days. This edition was beautifully printed and bound, with a new introduction by Francis Henry Taylor. The photographs had been made a few years earlier, and involved a few problems. To obtain interior views of the great vaulted refectories, halls, and crypts of Mont St. Michel, it was necessary to take long time exposures. The trouble was that this was the height of the tourist season, and as soon as I opened my shutter for a time exposure, a guide and a flock of visitors would appear upon the scene. After they moved on, I would open the shutter again, only to be interrupted by a new group of tourists. It was a frustrating experience until I had an inspiration, and hid in a remote corner while the monastery was locked up for a two-hour lunch period. Then I had the place to myself, and no further problems. Photographing the interior of Chartres Cathedral presented a similar puzzle, for people were walking through it at all times. I solved this by the long-established

Detail of the South Porch, Chartres, from *Mont St. Michel and Chartres*

179

The Chamberlains on the *Liberté*, with Stephanie and Narcisse

Pembroke, from *British Bouquet*

technique of stopping the lens opening down as far as possible, and allowing the shutter to stay open for about fifteen minutes. The passing throng was all but invisible, and the vaults and aisles of this very somber interior came out in clear detail.

Climbing the North Tower of Chartres Cathedral with a heavy view camera and film case presented another problem, but I toiled slowly up the interminable stone spiral staircases, and finally reached the topmost level open to visitors. The view of the exquisite Romanesque South Tower was breathtaking, and I made several hand-held shots of this and the complex flying buttresses far below. But if I ever make this climb again, it will be with a Leica!

The fourth chapter in Henry Adams's book deals with Normandy and the Île-de-France. He had his own strong favorites among the Romanesque churches of Normandy, and it was an exciting task to seek them out. We found that the tall spire of the church at Secqueville had just been repaired after suffering damage in World War II. The Abbey church at Cerisy-la-Foret and the church of Saint-Martin in Boscherville, both glorious, solid edifices, had escaped damage. The author spoke of the tiny village of Thaon and its Romanesque chapel, and this was a tough one. Even the most detailed maps failed to locate it, and the Norman country people to whom we spoke shook their

Weobley, from *British Bouquet*

heads in perplexity. Finally one ancient citizen gave us a clue, and we followed country roads that were hardly more than cowpaths to the deserted village. Its vine-grown chapel was just as lovely as Henry Adams said it would be.

Luckily for us he also mentioned about a dozen cathedrals in his text, giving us a fresh excuse to visit Amiens, Reims, Mantes, LeMans, Bayeux, Bourges, Caen, Toulouse, Auxerre, and Notre Dame de Paris. All of them appear among the illustrations.

Earle MacAusland, the publisher of *Gourmet,* has Scottish forebears, and is definitely pro-British. On numerous occasions he spoke to me about making a new series of epicurean articles on Britain. At first mention, this seemed a dubious idea, in view of the forlorn reputation of English cooking, and I hesitated for some time. But on second thought this presented something of a challenge, as well as a superb opportunity for another "traveling fellowship" in Britain. After all, some unrivaled delicacies are found in England—Whitstable oysters, Dover sole, Angus beef and Stilton cheese, for example. There are few dishes better than a steak and kidney pie when properly made, and the British are discriminating wine drinkers. London, of course, has some of the finest restaurants in the world. As an added inducement, Mr. MacAusland offered to use my color photographs to illustrate the articles, which were to be called "The Beauty of Britain."

The Hilltop, Kersey, from *British Bouquet*

The Almonry, Evesham, from *British Bouquet*

Land's End, Cornwall, from *British Bouquet*

John O'Groats, Scotland, from *British Bouquet*

Armed with notebooks, cameras and fat boxes of film, I sailed for France in the spring of 1959, acquired a new and more powerful Peugeot 403, and took a cross-channel steamer to Southampton. On a beautiful May morning I drove my shiny new car on the left-hand side of the road, and after a ridiculously short drive, was gazing at the Gothic splendor of Winchester cathedral. It was one of life's exciting moments.

My friends in London were hilarious when I told them of my plans. My old wartime associate, Major Tim Ashby, who imports Alsatian wines to London, was uproarious. "Listen, old boy, you're *not* going to attempt a Bouquet of Britain!" was the universal reaction. Nobody is as scornful of their own cooking as the British themselves! This was no time to be discouraged, and I bought all the available guidebooks on hotels and restaurants and set out for Cornwall. People talk about covering Britain, from Land's End in Cornwall to John O'Groats at the far tip of Scotland, and I was determined to do the same thing.

That summer of 1959 was blessed with beautiful weather, and I covered most of southwestern England in radiant sunshine. The heavy Linhof camera was a bit burdensome at times, but I worked it overtime in color as well as black-and-white. Cornwall and Devon are swamped with vacationists in summer, but in May the hotels were not crowded. I was able to stay in many of the best ones, and found surprisingly good food and wine in most of them. Gastronomy indeed

East Hagbourne, Berkshire, from *British Bouquet*

has its place in rural England! My summer's travels ended in the Cotswolds, which seemed totally unchanged since the days when Louis Skidmore and I had sketched our way through in 1928.

Great Britain may not be large, but it is concentrated, and closely packed with interest, and three additional summers were needed to complete the tour. My wife joined me in the quest in 1960 and 1961, and I covered the north of England and Scotland (including John O'Groats) alone in 1962. These three summers were far from consistently radiant, and it took a great deal of perseverance to get good photographs. Fortunately English skies are often not totally obscured. The weather reports mention "bright intervals," and these gave me a precious opportunity. A sudden burst of sunlight meant a dramatic picture set against a sodden sky of rain clouds. I have dozens of such photographs in the files, and they represent long vigils beside the tripod. Regardless of spots of bad weather, our British travels were wonderfully rewarding. The beauty of the castles, parish churches, manor houses and gardens scattered over England, and the warm friendliness of the people themselves is something that we shall never forget.

The first "Beauty of Britain" article on Cornwall appeared in the January, 1960, issue of *Gourmet,* accompanied by a large color picture, maps and black-and-white photographs. Other articles ran intermittently for three years, ending with a guide to London's choicer dining

Compton Wynyates, from *British Bouquet*

183

The High Street, Canterbury, frontispiece of *British Bouquet*

"Bright Interval" on the Village Green, Witney, from *British Bouquet*

places in September, 1963. During the winter months I rewrote and revised the text, and laid out the dummy for the new book which bore the title *British Bouquet*. My talented wife kitchen-tested and assembled a very creditable Treasury of British Recipes. The illustrations were mostly photographic, with the help of maps, vignettes and a few sketches. A drypoint and a pencil drawing served as end papers. This book was also printed in Denmark by Egmont H. Petersen, and ran to just six hundred pages. Bound in white with a British seal on the cover, it was published in the early autumn of 1963.

Summers were dedicated to travel in Britain, but other seasons of the year offered a chance to work on new projects. The most pressing and ambitious of these was a book to commemorate the twenty-fifth anniversary of Hastings House. It seemed hard to believe it, but their first book, *A Small House in the Sun,* had been published in 1936, and here we were in 1960. Walter Frese suggested a richly illustrated volume on New England that combined a cross section of my best pictures taken during that quarter century, whether they had been published or not. They were to be given ample captions, and most of the photographs were laid out to "bleed" to the edge of the page. A generous panorama of New England life was provided by the fourteen chapters, which dealt with the four seasons in New England, its farms, villages, towns, rivers and lakes, churches, institutions of learning, early inns and taverns, mills, historic houses, doorways, interiors and

The Fishing Village of Crail, Scotland, from *British Bouquet*

185

The Royall House, Medford, Massachusetts, from *The New England Image*

Summer Afternoon in Northwood, New Hampshire, from *The New England Image*

the coastline from Connecticut to West Quoddy Head, Maine. There was also a chapter on literary New England from Anne Bradstreet to Emily Dickinson, all told in pictures.

It took an interminable time to assemble all these photographs, lay them out, and write the captions, and I missed the anniversary date. *The New England Image* appeared one year late, in 1962, but few readers noticed my tardiness. Artistically this is surely the best of all my photographic books. This is largely due to the superb gravure work of the printers, Conzett & Huber, of Zurich, Switzerland. Their reproductions have a marvelous richness and depth of detail. Part of this fine quality is due to the fact that I supplied them with negatives of all the selected subjects. Working from a negative instead of a glossy print, the Swiss technicians could bring out hidden details, clarify dark areas and hold back glaring highlights. The result is a large book of a hundred and ninety-two pages that glows with light and animation, and made the author and publisher glow with considerable happiness also.

These negatives came from ever-expanding filing cabinets that grew higher and higher in my studio over the grocery store. I should have explained long ago that it was not a fully equipped photographer's

Doorway of the Nickels-Sortwell House, Wiscasset, Maine, from *The New England Image*

Sailing Vessel in Wickford, Rhode Island

Corner Cupboard in Darien, Connecticut

From *The New England Image*

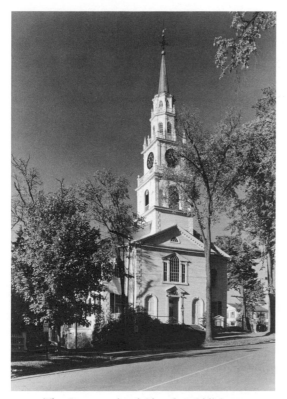

The Congregational Church, Middlebury,
Vermont, from *The New England Image*

studio. It had no darkroom. I have never attempted to practice all the phases of the photographer's art—developing and printing, for example. Life is just too short, with all the travel, writing and layout that my book work entails. So I have always farmed out the laboratory work. For the past twenty years or so a gifted technician named Eric Muller has solved my darkroom problems, producing fine clean negatives, contact prints and enlargements. He came to New England from Sweden many years ago, and has the European's love of his *metier,* insistence upon quality, and the capacity of infinite patience.

The field work, however, is all my own, and frequently I have been asked to explain my photographic technique. The answer is so simple that it disappoints some questioners. All of my best pictures are made with a 5 x 7 Linhof view camera, set on a tripod and leveled with a small pocket level. The picture is focused and composed on the ground glass with the aid of the classic black focusing cloth. Using only one type of fast film, two different yellow filters, and a sensitive exposure meter, I am free from some of the complications that worry more sophisticated photographers.

Composition, of course, assumes vast importance in photography, and my artistic training has been a help here. I rarely take a picture unless I "see" it first with the naked eye. Values are equally essential, and a center of interest can make or break a picture. Sunlight is a price-

The Old Meeting House, Hancock, New Hampshire, from *The New England Image*

less ingredient in outdoor photography, and I rarely venture forth without it. Cross lighting is almost obligatory, for there is nothing duller than a photograph taken with the sunlight directly behind the camera. A good subject deserves to be viewed from several angles. It should be "stalked" if circumstances permit. Photography demands a great deal of footwork! Usually I take a good subject from several angles, and then use the best one.

Skies are of immense importance. A filter will bring out the sky values, of course, especially if clouds are in evidence. If the sky is blank, I try to screen it with branches or foliage at the top of the picture. A blank foreground is equally dull, and this can usually be solved by diligent footwork. I employ every possible manoeuvre to circumvent the brash intrusion of utility poles and wires. All seasons of the year are fitting for the observant camera, of course, but spring and fall are more favorable to the outdoor cameraman. The first blush of spring foliage is the happiest moment of all. Summer foliage is likely to be blackish and lifeless in pictures, but the seashore and the lakes are incomparable then. Winter has the glorious advantage of covering up thousands of ugly composition asphalt roofs with a clean layer of snow.

The Battle Green, Lexington, Massachusetts

Ospedale del Ceppo, Pistoia,
from *The Flavor of Italy*

Tour de l'Horloge, Auxerre,
from *The Flavor of France*

An Umbrian gateway, from *Italian Bouquet*

There is certainly no rule of thumb about the best time of day to take pictures. High noon is rarely the right moment, however. I have never "dubbed in" skies, and do not like to crop negatives to make a good composition: Instead I try to compose the pictures on the ground glass of the camera, just as an artist would fill a canvas. No two photographers apply the same technique, of course, and some of my ideas may seem a trifle archaic. But here they are.

Two volumes of a gay little cookbook called *The Flavor of France* have also appeared in the sixties, as mentioned earlier in these pages. Each page contains a photogenic view of France under which is a carefully worded recipe. This is a family affair, originated by our daughter Narcisse. She wrote the introduction and edited the books. My wife selected the recipes and tested them, while I supplied the pictures. A similar volume, *The Flavor of Italy,* appeared in 1965. These three books have been popular in Great Britain, but we had to make up a special jacket and title page for Hamish Hamilton, the publisher. This is because he could never offer a book in England with "Flavor" spelt the American way. So his edition is emblazoned "Flavour," and Mr. Hamilton refers to them as "the U and non-U editions."

The *Sampler of American Cooking* appeared in 1961, in the same format. These four volumes were all compiled from engagement calendars that appeared annually over the years.

The Abbey Farm, from *Bouquet de France*

Time has a way of galloping along, and it had become evident for years that *Bouquet de France* was becoming a bit outdated. Published in 1952, it listed many hotels and dining places that have inevitably faded away. Owners and chefs retire, sell out, or pass on to their rewards. Their wives elope, their blood pressures rise, their creditors close in, or their culinary standards slump. Now and then we received indignant letters from readers who had made a special detour to visit a restaurant we had raved about, only to find that it had been closed for years. The time seemed ripe, even imperative, for a completely new volume, recording the changes that had taken place in French life, travel and gastronomy. We decided to embark on a new series of articles for *Gourmet* under the title of "France Revisited."

This pilgrimage began in Normandy and Brittany in the northeastern corner of France, and progressed in a leisurely clockwise fashion around the entire country. This time we didn't exactly travel incognito. Our hosts recognized us in many cases, and rolled out the red carpet. *Bouquet de France* had been supplying them with discriminating American and British clients for years, and at no cost whatsoever to the owners. Most publicity has a price tag in France, but here was

Grand Puits, from *Bouquet de France*

191

The Château, Bioule-Négrepelisse, from *Bouquet de France*

Lisieux, from *Bouquet de France*

an exception, and our recommended hotel and restaurant owners went out of their way to be cordial. We were wined and banqueted, and sometimes sent away with gifts of old brandy, *foie gras,* chocolates, lace and perfume, not to mention an occasional case of wine for our roadside picnics. It wasn't easy to follow my doctor's stern orders, which were to go easy on the calories!

Besides old friends, there were any number of new restaurants to explore. Normandy had been rebuilt, and Caen, Evreux and Le Havre possessed fine new ultramodern shrines of gastronomy. The picture had changed in Alsace too, and a whole new constellation of restaurants glittered on the French Riviera. In Paris the superlative standbys, Grand Vefour, Maxim's, Laperouse, La Tour d'Argent, Lasserre and Lucas Carton still put forth their expensive best, but there were exciting newcomers such as Chez Garin and Chez les Anges.

There were ample opportunities to use my Linhof camera, refurbished after a bad fall with its tripod, and for the sketch pad as well. "France Revisited" ran for two and a half years in *Gourmet,* and we made three trips of varying lengths to complete our notes and pictures. The new *Bouquet de France* is almost unrecognizable from its predecessor, with an entirely new layout, new sketches and photographs (only about a dozen were held over) and a vastly revised text. It has the plumpness that becomes a gastronomic book, and runs to six hundred and eighty-six pages. The "Treasury of Regional Recipes" is more opulent than ever. The printing, once again, was done in the

Château de Victot-Pontfol,
from *Bouquet de France*

193

Albi, on the River Tarn, from *Bouquet de France*

The Banks of the Yonne, Auxerre,
from *Bouquet de France*

duotone offset process by Egmont H. Petersen in Copenhagen. We had an opportunity to visit this extraordinary plant, the foremost in Denmark, during a Scandinavian cruise in the autumn of 1966. We met all of the department heads who had worked on our three books. Each of them spoke fluent English, and greeted us as old friends. We have never seen such an immaculate printing plant. All of the staff wore pristine white dusters. Everything was spotless, especially the rows of ten wash basins for printers' supposedly soiled hands. We visited the photographic department where so many of my pictures had been reproduced, and admired the huge camera and developing plant, which turned out to be of American manufacture.

Egmont H. Petersen, the modest founder of this extraordinary enterprise, left this world decades ago, we were told. The plant expands constantly under his name, and besides being the official government printer, handles such important undertakings as printing the telephone books and stock certificates. Color printing is a specialty, and many foreign publications rely heavily upon this firm for their color work.

We had luncheon on the top floor of the building with members of the staff. A plump Danish cook brought us schnapps and beer, open sandwiches, pastry and coffee. Later the General Manager of the firm, Mr. Arne Byskov, gave us a fastidious dinner at the Maritime Restaurant. Our enthusiasm for the Danes is boundless.

The new book has end papers made from pencil drawings, and each

194

Manoir d'Archelles, from *Bouquet de France*

of the twenty-eight chapters is introduced by a full-page bleed photograph. There are maps and vignettes as before, but no calligraphy. Binding problems delayed the publication date until November, but the new *Bouquet de France* burst into view in the bookstores in time for the Christmas shoppers. It is by far our most ambitious book, and I think we will taper off after this. Never have I worked so hard, especially while making up the dummy of this fattening book.

After twenty-one years, my studio over Osborne's grocery store had filled up to an alarming degree. Practically nothing had been thrown away. So many bookshelves of pamphlets and guide books had built up that I had to stack one in front of the other. The Piranesi and Decaris engravings on the walls had been largely obscured by rising stacks of negative files. My etching press was all but invisible under piles of portfolios, blotters, and solander boxes. There was also an attractive little upright Broadwood piano that had once been installed in the Duke of Northumberland's yacht in Cannes. We had bought it at a French auction, and somehow it had found its way to this studio. It made a useful bookcase, and was so covered with books and documents that it was completely invisible to the human eye.

The moment of decision was at hand. I either had to clean house or move. Something *had* to be done, and I solved it by buying the commodious studio of a landscape painter on Marblehead's Washington Street. Details of the housemoving are too harrowing to be recorded. I sold my etching press to a graphic artist in Pennsylvania, and de-

Amiens Cathedral, from *Bouquet de France*

A corner of the studio over Osborne's Grocery Store (photograph by Gregory Smith)

Abbot Hall Hill in Midwinter, from *Old Marblehead*

posited at least a ton of old correspondence, canceled checks, defective enlargements and mere trash in the Marblehead incinerator. Before the decisive move to new quarters was made, Gregory Smith, an observant amateur photographer, came up to the studio with his Rolleflex, and recorded its magnificent chaos. He made a book of enlargements of the scene, and one of them is reproduced here.

The new quarters are roomy and flooded with sunlight on a clear day. A huge bookcase fills one end of the studio and provides space for my collection of reference books on France, Italy, Britain, food, wine, and architecture. The negative files are in a smaller room, stacked neatly and labeled. How many negatives are stored here? A good guess would be seventy thousand, most of them 5 x 7 cut film in manila envelopes. Many of them have a certain historic interest because they show New England before the advent of parking meters, television antennae and too many parked automobiles. Then there is the recipe collection, patiently typed on 4 x 6-inch cards by my secretary, Ruth Krenz, over a period of fourteen years. It consists of forty metal files on French, Italian and American cooking. There are neat cabinets for drawings, etchings, photographic enlargements and contact prints. Order has been restored, and at last I'm proud to receive visitors.

This brings us down to time, as the announcers say, and I see that my half century is up, and then some. These have been decades of rather mild adventure, with few of the dashing exploits of professional

Mason Street, Marblehead

197

Race Week, from *Old Marblehead*

The Scotch-Boardman House,
Saugus, Massachusetts

journalists. Still, my fifty years have involved two wars, and a great deal of travel and picture making. I haven't the foggiest notion of how many times we have crossed the Atlantic, or how many tires we have worn out motoring over European roads, or the number of sketches, prints and photographs that have accumulated from all this activity. I can only promise you that it has been a happy and rewarding experience.

Although gastronomy has sometimes tried to elbow the graphic arts out of position, I have been steadfast in a devotion to architecture and draftsmanship. The tradition of English, French and American black-and-white artists of the past century has influenced my work far more than the contemporary trend in the graphic arts. Not that more imaginative art fails to enthuse our household. I would love to be able to paint a Bonnard still life or a Cézanne landscape if I could. But there is a public for representational drawings, etchings and photographs, and it isn't limited to the dear little lady in the white hat who patronizes summer art galleries. Enough letters from architects, draftsmen, travelers and book collectors have accumulated to make me feel that all these years of scurrying about have not been wasted. If we have brought them pleasure, and a glimpse of beauty now and then, and perhaps a new and delicious dish to try in their kitchens, our reward has been more than ample.

Meanwhile a new "traveling fellowship" is perhaps in the offing. If *le bon Dieu* is willing, an illustrated volume on Burgundy, its Romanesque churches, brick manor houses, regional cookery and magnificent wines, would represent a joyous and worthwhile undertaking. And the faithful grey Peugeot 403 is still waiting in Le Havre.

Appendices

A Sicilian and His Donkey,
from *Italian Bouquet*

Preceding page:
Detail of Cathedral Doors by Barisano di Trani, Ravello,
from *Italian Bouquet*

Cascia, from *Italian Bouquet*

Published Etchings, Drypoints and Lithographs, and Commissioned Prints

BY SAMUEL CHAMBERLAIN, N.A.

Plate dimensions include plate marks, and are indicated with the vertical measurement
always first. One hundred ninety-nine prints are listed, including (in brief
exception to the title of this list) a very few unpublished prints.

Title	Date	Medium	Dimensions	Edition
Vingt Lithographies du Vieux Paris, issued as a portfolio:				
Cour de Dragon, Paris	1924	lithograph	13½ x 8½	100
Le Dome de l'Église du Vale-de-Grace, Paris	1924	lithograph	16⅞ x 10¼	100
Échoppe d'Étameur, Paris	1924	lithograph	11¼ x 13¼	100
L'Épicerie, Rue Grande, Paris	1924	lithograph	15½ x 9¼	100
Fontaine de la Grosse Horloge, Rouen	1924	lithograph	17 X 11	100
L'Horloge, Paris	1924	lithograph	14¼ x 8¾	100
Maison de la Tourelle, Rue des Francs Bourgeois, Paris	1924	lithograph	14½ x 10¼	100
La Maison du Saumon, Chartres	1924	lithograph	13¼ X 11	100
Passy Ancien et Nouveau, Paris	1924	lithograph	12½ x 11¼	100
Un Portail de l'Église de St. Étienne du Mont, Paris	1924	lithograph	15½ x 10¼	100
Porte St. Martin, Paris	1924	lithograph	8¾ x 17⅞	100
Rue de l'Abbaye, Paris	1924	lithograph	14⅝ x 9	100
Rue de la Bucherie, Paris	1924	lithograph	10¾ x 12	100
Rue de la Montagne, St. Geneviève, Paris	1924	lithograph	15¾ x 10	100

Church of St. Ayoul, Provins

201

The Curiosity Shop, Paris

The Winding Road, Vernon

Title	*Date*	*Medium*	*Dimensions*	*Edition*
Rue du Dragon, Paris	1924	lithograph	9 x 13	100
Rue Fréderic–Sauton, Paris	1924	lithograph	12¾ x 9¼	100
Rue Saint Severin, Paris	1924	lithograph	15¾ x 10	100
Saint Nicolas-des-Champs, Paris	1924	lithograph	14 x 8¾	100
Le Vase du Panthéon, Paris	1924	lithograph	14½ x 10½	100
Vieille Maison, Rue St. Étienne-du-Mont, Paris	1924	lithograph	14¼ x 11	100
A Sidestreet in Beauvais (First published etching—First Honorable Mention, Paris Salon, 1925)	1925	etching	13¼ x 9⅜	100
The Ile-de-la-Cité, Paris	1925	etching	10¾ x 11¾	82
The Blacksmith's Shop, Senlis	1925	etching	8¾ x 11⅛	22
Old Houses in Rouen	1925	etching	10⅛ x 7¾	13
The Loggia di Lanzi, Florence	1925	etching	11¼ x 7⅝	33
Taormina	1925	etching	10⅞ x 7⅛	20
The Buttresses of Beauvais Cathedral	1925	etching	8⅞ x 5	100
Amalfi	1925	etching	7 x 7	96
The Curiosity Shop, Paris	1925	etching	5½ x 7⅜	33
Church of San Giovanni Battiste, Siracusa	1925	etching	5½ x 6⅜	36
Church of St. Ayoul, Provins	1925	etching	5¾ x 7¾	68
The Church at Sezanne	1925	etching	7¾ x 3¾	100
Semur-en-Auxois	1925	etching	6¼ x 9⅜	32
A Gateway in Seville	1925	etching	7⅞ x 5¼	32
Gateway of Santa Maria, Burgos	1925	etching	6 x 4¾	35
Houses on the River, Albi	1925	etching	5⅞ x 4⅛	20
Old Houses in Lisieux	1925	soft-ground etching	7½ x 4⅝	28
The Cypresses, Siracusa	1925	soft-ground etching	7¼ x 8⅜	61
The Giant Buttress, Bourges	1925	soft-ground etching	7⅝ x 5⅝	14
The Fish Market, Chartres (First Honorable Mention, Paris Salon, 1925)	1925	soft-ground etching	7⅜ x 10⅞	49
The Bridge of Pinos, Spain (First published drypoint)	1925	drypoint	3⅛ x 5¼	12
Springtime in Senlis	1925	drypoint	7⅞ x 9⅜	20
The Rue Daubenton, Paris	1925	drypoint	8⅛ x 5½	15
The Beach, Minori	1925	drypoint	5⅛ x 6½	15
The Rue Mouffetard, Paris	1925	lithograph	9½ x 15¼	35
The Cloister, St. Benoit	1925	lithograph	3¾ x 8	13
The Tower in Andujar	1925	lithograph	13 x 10	25
Chateaudun	1925	lithograph	7¼ x 9⅛	25
The Chateau in the Lot	1925	lithograph	3½ x 7½	25
Gateway in Perpignan	1925	lithograph	11⅛ x 7⅛	20
Montrichard in May	1926	drypoint	6 3/16 x 4¾	20
The Farm Gate, Virolet	1926	drypoint on zinc	7⅛ x 5	15
The Poplars	1926	drypoint on zinc	5⅛ x 6⅞	10
Vitré	1926	drypoint	3⅞ x 6	75
The Kitchen Door	1926	drypoint	4½ x 6¼	60
The Winding Road, Vernon	1926	drypoint	8 x 5⅞	50
The Porches, Dinan	1926	drypoint	8⅜ x 5⅞	50
Remnants of Gothic Lacework	1926	drypoint	8⅞ x 4⅜	50
The Village Church, Menilles	1926	drypoint on zinc	7 x 5⅛	10
The Hilltop, Villefranche	1926	drypoint	4⅛ x 4 13/16	60
A Gateway in Toledo	1926	etching	6 x 4	

Title	Date	Medium	Dimensions	Edi-tion
(Plate made for the frontispiece of "The Print Connoisseur" for April 1926)				
A Study of Trees	1926	drypoint	5 x 7	50
(Plate made for "The Graphic Processes" by Louis A. Holman)				
Vieilles Maisons, Dinan	1927	lithograph	7½ x 10½	35
The Quais, St. Tropez	1927	drypoint	4¼ x 4¹³⁄₁₆	60
The Waterfront, Villefranche	1927	drypoint	5⅛ x 7	75
The Battered Boat, Villefranche	1927	drypoint	4⅜ x 6⅜	75
Old Menton	1927	drypoint	7 x 5	75
The Sheltered Street, Vitré	1927	lithograph	9¼ x 12¾	10
Petite Venise, Colmar	1927	drypoint	5 x 7	60
Broom Shop, Lucca	1927	lithograph	5¾ x 9⅛	50
Cathedral Spires, Angers	1927	drypoint	9⅛ x 5¾	75
The Veterans, Josselin	1927	drypoint	4⁵⁄₁₆ x 7	75
Porte du Vieux Pont, Sospel	1928	lithograph	6 x 9	50
Siena	1928	drypoint	12⅜ x 6¼	100
Gables of Colmar	1928	drypoint	8¹⁄₁₆ x 10⅞	100
Plaza San Martin, Segovia	1928	drypoint	6⁵⁄₁₆ x 7¾	100
Perugia	1928	drypoint	12½ x 7¾	100
Cour du Marché, Bruges	1928	drypoint	8⅞ x 6⅜	100
The Sunlit Tower, Colmar	1928	drypoint	14 x 7¾	100
Sailors Home from the Sea	1928	drypoint	6¾ x 9¾	100
Broad Street, Ludlow	1928	drypoint	7¾ x 10¹⁄₁₆	100
Canterbury	1928	drypoint	9⅜ x 6⅞	100
A Stable Court in Essex	1928	drypoint	7⅜ x 9¾	100
Founder's Tower, Oxford	1928	drypoint	11 x 7	100
An Umbrian Gateway	1928	lithograph	8¾ x 6⁵⁄₁₆	10
A Farm Group in the Tuscan Hills	1928	drypoint	5⅝ x 8⅞	few proofs
Harness Shop	1928	drypoint	4 x 6	50
Lucca	1928	lithograph	9⅝ x 6⅛	25
The Market Place, Bourges	1928	etching	6¾ x 4¹¹⁄₁₆	more than 3,000
(Published as frontispiece of *Domestic Architecture in Rural France*)				
The Tontine Crescent, Franklin Place, Boston	1928	drypoint	6¾ x 5⅜	100
(Presentation plate made for the Iconographic Society)				
Salamanca Cathedral	1929	drypoint	10⅞ x 7⅛	100
Hôpital St. Jean, Bruges	1929	drypoint	8⅜ x 9⅛	100
Far West Junk Shop	1929	drypoint	4⅝ x 8¾	100
Soaring Steel	1929	drypoint	12½ x 9⅝	100
Manhattan, Old and New	1929	drypoint	9 x 7	100
Boston Fish Pier	1929	drypoint	5⅝ x 8⅝	100
Faneuil Hall, Boston	1929	drypoint	6¼ x 9	100
The Customs Tower, Boston	1929	drypoint	5⅝ x 8	few proofs
Drizzly Morning in Chicago	1929	drypoint	4 x 7½	100
The Curving Canyon, New York	1929	drypoint	8⅞ x 5⅞	100
Verneuil	1929	drypoint	13⅞ x 8	100
The City Cross, Winchester	1929	etching	9⁵⁄₁₆ x 6½	more than 3,000
(Published as frontispiece of *Tudor Homes of England*)				
La Charité-Sur-Loire	1930	drypoint	11¾ x 8¼	100
Market Day in Lillebonne	1930	drypoint	13⅞ x 9³⁄₁₆	100
Auxerre	1930	drypoint	6⅛ x 8½	75
Slums of Rouen	1930	drypoint	8 x 5⅞	few proofs

The Kitchen Door, Vernon

Village Street in Vitré

Winter in Concord, Massachusetts
Pencil Points cover, December 1935

Title	Date	Medium	Dimensions	Edition
Farm Vista, Le Plessis-Luzarches	1930	drypoint	$8\frac{3}{8}$ x $6\frac{5}{8}$	few proofs
Dentelles Gothiques, Clamecy	1930	drypoint	$15\frac{1}{8}$ x $10\frac{1}{8}$	100
Cathedral of Sens	1930	drypoint	$10\frac{3}{4}$ x $7\frac{1}{8}$	100
Skyscrapers of Menton	1930	drypoint	$12\frac{3}{4}$ x $9\frac{7}{16}$	100
Towers of Senlis	1930	drypoint	10 x $7\frac{1}{4}$	100
Gateway in the Ghetto, Paris	1930	drypoint	$7\frac{5}{8}$ x $4\frac{7}{8}$	100
Midsummer Silhouette	1930	drypoint	$5\frac{7}{8}$ x $5\frac{3}{4}$	75
The Shadowy Street	1930	drypoint	$4\frac{7}{8}$ x $4\frac{1}{2}$	75
Fruit Store Façade	1930	drypoint	$4\frac{5}{8}$ x $6\frac{3}{16}$	75
Place Notre Dame, Senlis	1930	drypoint	$5\frac{11}{16}$ x $6\frac{1}{4}$	75
The Mason's House, Senlis	1930	drypoint	$10\frac{3}{8}$ x 8	100
Porte St. Guillaume, Chartres	1930	drypoint	$7\frac{7}{8}$ x $6\frac{3}{16}$	100
Chartres Cathedral	1931	drypoint	$14\frac{3}{8}$ x $9\frac{3}{16}$	100
Beauvais	1931	drypoint	$11\frac{5}{16}$ x $12\frac{1}{4}$	100
Silhouette of Senlis	1931	drypoint	$5\frac{7}{8}$ x $8\frac{5}{8}$	100
The Verdant Village	1931	drypoint	$6\frac{3}{4}$ x $11\frac{1}{8}$	100
The Saplings	1931	drypoint	$7\frac{9}{16}$ x $10\frac{5}{16}$	100
The Abbey Farm	1931	drypoint	$7\frac{3}{4}$ x $10\frac{3}{8}$	100
College St. Vincent, Senlis	1931	drypoint	$4\frac{5}{16}$ x $5\frac{1}{4}$	few proofs
Senlis from a Crow's Nest	1931	drypoint	$11\frac{3}{8}$ x $9\frac{5}{8}$	100
Manhattan Twilight	1932	etching	$13\frac{5}{16}$ x $9\frac{9}{16}$	100
Espalion	1933	drypoint	$6\frac{1}{2}$ x 11	75
Lisieux	1933	drypoint	$6\frac{7}{8}$ x 11	75
Albi Sunset	1933	drypoint	$9\frac{3}{8}$ x $11\frac{5}{8}$	100
The Country Road	1933	drypoint	8 x $10\frac{3}{8}$	75
The Abbey of Montmajour	1934	drypoint	8 x $11\frac{5}{16}$	75
Hospital Santa Cruz, Toledo (Presentation plate made for the Rochester, New York, Print Club)	c. 1934	drypoint	$9\frac{3}{16}$ x $7\frac{7}{8}$	about 300

Twelve Etchings of Yale, issued as a portfolio:

Title	Date	Medium	Dimensions	Edition
Bingham Hall and Hale Statue	1934	drypoint	$11\frac{7}{8}$ x $8\frac{1}{4}$	125
Calhoun College	1934	drypoint	$8\frac{1}{8}$ x $9\frac{7}{8}$	125
Davenport College	1934	drypoint	$9\frac{9}{16}$ x $9\frac{7}{8}$	125
Divinity School Quadrangle	1934	drypoint	$6\frac{1}{4}$ x $9\frac{1}{2}$	125
Graduate School	1934	drypoint	$11\frac{1}{2}$ x $7\frac{7}{8}$	125
Harkness Memorial Tower	1934	drypoint	$13\frac{9}{16}$ x $9\frac{15}{16}$	125
Jonathan Edwards College	1934	drypoint	$11\frac{9}{16}$ x $7\frac{1}{16}$	125
Payne Whitney Gymnasium	1934	drypoint	12 x $8\frac{1}{2}$	125
Pierson College	1934	drypoint	$10\frac{1}{8}$ x $6\frac{7}{8}$	125
Sheffield Scientific School Tower	1934	drypoint	$10\frac{1}{2}$ x $7\frac{5}{8}$	125
Sterling Law Buildings	1934	drypoint	$8\frac{15}{16}$ x $11\frac{5}{8}$	125
University Library Entrance Portal	1934	drypoint	$10\frac{9}{16}$ x $7\frac{5}{8}$	125
The Abandoned Chateau	1935	drypoint	$7\frac{7}{8}$ x $9\frac{3}{4}$	100
Quimper	1935	drypoint	$14\frac{5}{8}$ x $8\frac{3}{4}$	100
The Giant Oak	1935	drypoint	$8\frac{5}{8}$ x $10\frac{1}{4}$	100
Burgundy Hillside	1935	drypoint	$9\frac{1}{8}$ x $11\frac{1}{8}$	100
Continental Illinois Bank and Trust Company (Private commission)	c. 1935	drypoint	$14\frac{3}{8}$ x $11\frac{11}{16}$	100
Pembroke (Demonstration plate)	c. 1935	etching	$5\frac{3}{16}$ x $7\frac{3}{16}$	few proofs
The Hilltop, Kersey	c. 1935	etching	$6\frac{1}{8}$ x $7\frac{7}{8}$	few proofs

Nine prints executed for use as covers for "Pencil Points" Magazine:

Title	Date	Medium	Dimensions	Edition
Boston Courtyard	1935	drypoint	6 x $3\frac{1}{8}$	few proofs

Title	Date	Medium	Dimensions	Edi-tion
Mission Courtyard	1935	drypoint	$5\frac{15}{16}$ x $3\frac{1}{16}$	few proofs
Apse of St. John the Divine, New York	1935	drypoint	6 x $3\frac{1}{8}$	few proofs
The Derelicts, Rockland, Maine	1935	drypoint	$5\frac{7}{8}$ x $3\frac{1}{16}$	few proofs
Central Park, New York	1935	drypoint	6 x $3\frac{1}{8}$	few proofs
Concord in Winter	1935	drypoint	6 x $3\frac{1}{8}$	few proofs
The "Scotch"-Boardman House, Saugus, Massachusetts	1936	drypoint	$3\frac{7}{16}$ x $3\frac{7}{8}$	few proofs
Fisherman's Shanty, Marblehead, Massachusetts	1936	drypoint	$4\frac{1}{8}$ x $4\frac{5}{8}$	few proofs
Soviet Housing Development	1936	drypoint	$4\frac{5}{8}$ x 5	few proofs
Essex Village	1936	drypoint	$6\frac{3}{16}$ x $11\frac{11}{16}$	100
Noon in Noyers	1936	drypoint	$7\frac{5}{8}$ x $8\frac{7}{8}$	100
Summer Street, Marblehead (Arms Award at the Society of American Etchers Annual Exhibition)	1936	drypoint	$9\frac{3}{8}$ x $7\frac{1}{8}$	100
Stonington Sunset	1936	drypoint	$9\frac{7}{8}$ x $14\frac{5}{8}$	100
Saunderstown Fields	1936	drypoint	$7\frac{3}{16}$ x $10\frac{5}{8}$	100
Bank of New York and Trust Company (Private commission)	c. 1936	drypoint	$10\frac{1}{2}$ x $5\frac{1}{2}$	few proofs
New England Hill Town (Old Marblehead from Crocker Park)	1937	drypoint	$10\frac{1}{8}$ x $13\frac{1}{8}$	few proofs
Sunshine After Showers—The Nantucket, 1937	1937	drypoint	$8\frac{3}{8}$ x $12\frac{1}{8}$	12
Springtime in Salem (Voted most popular print at the New York World's Fair, 1940)	1938	drypoint	$8\frac{7}{8}$ x $12\frac{1}{8}$	100
The Rogers Building, MIT	1938	drypoint	$12\frac{3}{16}$ x $9\frac{1}{8}$	100
Christ Church, Cambridge	1938	drypoint	12 x $9\frac{1}{4}$	100
Mediterranean Village— Villefranche-Sur-Mer (Presentation plate for the New Haven, Connecticut, Print Club)	1938	drypoint	$8\frac{7}{16}$ x $11\frac{3}{4}$	about 300
The Apothecary's Shop, Williamsburg	1938	drypoint	$9\frac{1}{8}$ x $7\frac{1}{4}$	100
The Capitol, Williamsburg	1938	drypoint	$9\frac{5}{8}$ x $14\frac{1}{4}$	100
The Governor's Palace, Williamsburg	1938	drypoint	$10\frac{1}{4}$ x $14\frac{5}{8}$	100
The Raleigh Tavern, Williamsburg	1938	drypoint	$8\frac{7}{8}$ x $12\frac{1}{4}$	100
Bruton Parish Church, Williamsburg	1938	drypoint	$10\frac{1}{2}$ x $7\frac{1}{2}$	100
The Public Gaol, Williamsburg	1938	drypoint	$7\frac{3}{4}$ x 11	100
The Palace Gardens, Williamsburg	1939	drypoint	$9\frac{3}{8}$ x $13\frac{1}{4}$	100
Mediterranean Wash Day	1939	drypoint	9 x $12\frac{3}{4}$	27
Bend in the Road	1939	drypoint	$7\frac{3}{8}$ x $13\frac{3}{8}$	75
Early Morning Market, Senlis (Presentation plate made for the Society of American Etchers)	1939	drypoint	$9\frac{1}{8}$ x $6\frac{3}{4}$	about 300
St. George Tucker House, Williamsburg	1940	drypoint	$9\frac{1}{2}$ x $7\frac{1}{4}$	100
Valley of the Var	1940	drypoint	$10\frac{13}{16}$ x $13\frac{3}{16}$	25
Summer Shadows (Presentation print for Friends of Contemporary Prints, Marble-head, Massachusetts)	1940	drypoint	$8\frac{5}{8}$ x $11\frac{1}{8}$	300

Derelicts in Rockland, Maine
Pencil Points cover, October 1935

Chateau de Creil, Oise

Cloisters of the Cathedral, Angers

Title	Date	Medium	Dimensions	Edition
The King Hooper Mansion (Demonstration plate)	1940	soft-ground etching	$7\frac{3}{16} \times 5\frac{3}{16}$	few proofs
Butcher Row, Coventry (Published as frontispiece for the de luxe edition of *This Realm, This England*)	1941	drypoint	$7\frac{3}{8} \times 5\frac{7}{8}$	300
Old Nassau Hall, Princeton (Print made for the Princeton Print Club)	1946	drypoint	$11\frac{3}{8} \times 8\frac{1}{8}$	about 300
Harborside, Friendship, Maine (Presentation print made for the Chicago Society of Etchers)	1946	drypoint	$8\frac{11}{16} \times 12\frac{11}{16}$	about 300
The Semple House, Williamsburg	1946	drypoint	$8\frac{3}{8} \times 7\frac{1}{4}$	125
Jacquemart, Moulins (Presentation plate made for the Rockford, Illinois, Print Club)	1948	drypoint	$13\frac{3}{8} \times 8\frac{11}{16}$	about 100
The Churchyard, Williamsburg	1948	drypoint	$6\frac{7}{8} \times 9\frac{1}{4}$	62
Harvard Hall (Plate made for the Harvard Club of Boston)	c. 1948	drypoint	$9\frac{5}{8} \times 8$	100
The Front Door (Plate made for the Harvard Club of Boston)	c. 1948	drypoint	$8\frac{11}{16} \times 5\frac{5}{8}$	100
Memorial Chapel—Nashville, Tennessee (Private commission)	c. 1949	drypoint	$6\frac{1}{2} \times 11$	50
Barnegat Cottage—Marblehead (Presentation print for the Friends of Contemporary Prints, Marblehead, Massachusetts)	c. 1949	drypoint	$7\frac{15}{16} \times 11\frac{1}{4}$	300
The First National Bank Building, Boston (Private commission)	1949	drypoint	$10\frac{3}{16} \times 9\frac{5}{8}$	about 10
Saugus Iron Works (Commission Plate for the Saugus Ironworks Association)	1958	drypoint	$7\frac{1}{8} \times 11\frac{1}{8}$	300

The Domes of San Giovanni degli Eremiti
Palermo

Towers of Cairo

Books Written or Illustrated, 1924-1967

BY SAMUEL CHAMBERLAIN

Two portfolios of prints are included in the list. One or two revised editions
of particular books are listed separately, to keep the chronological
sequence of various undertakings.

Vingt Lithographies du Vieux Paris (1924). Portfolio published by the artist.

Sketches of Northern Spanish Architecture (1925). Published by Architectural
Book Publishing Company, New York.

Domestic Architecture in Rural France (1928). Architectural Book Publishing
Company.

Tudor Homes of England (1929). Architectural Book Publishing Company.

Through France with a Sketchbook (1929). Robert M. McBride & Company,
New York.

Twelve Etchings of Yale (1934). Portfolio published under the sponsorship of
Yale University.

A Small House in the Sun (1936). Hastings House, Publishers, Inc., New York.

Cape Cod in the Sun (1937). Hastings House.

Open House in New England (1937). Stephen Daye Press, Brattleboro, Vermont.

Sagra di San Michele

Beyond New England Thresholds (1938). Hastings House.

Historic Salem in Four Seasons (1938). Hastings House.

Gloucester and Cape Ann (1938). Hastings House.

Historic Boston in Four Seasons (1938). Hastings House.

Church of Notre-Dame, Dôle,
from *Bouquet de France*

Marina Grande, Capri,
from *Italian Bouquet*

Longfellow's Wayside Inn (1938). Hastings House.

Lexington and Concord (1939). Hastings House.

Nantucket (1939). Hastings House.

New England Doorways (1939). Hastings House.

Old Marblehead (1940). Hastings House.

Portsmouth, New Hampshire (1940). Hastings House.

France Will Live Again (1940). Hastings House. (Introduction by Donald Moffat.)

Martha's Vineyard (1941). Hastings House.

This Realm, This England (1941). Hastings House. (Introduction by Donald Moffat.)

The Coast of Maine (1941). Hastings House.

Fair Is Our Land (1942). Hastings House. (Introduction by Donald Moffat.)

Historic Cambridge in Four Seasons (1942). Hastings House.

The Old Bay Paths (1942). Hastings House. (Text by George Francis Marlowe.)

The Education of Henry Adams (1942). The Limited Editions Club. (Etched illustrations only.)

Clementine in the Kitchen (1943). Hastings House. (Published under the *nom de plume* of Phineas Beck.)

Ever New England (1944). Hastings House. (Introduction by Donald Moffat.)

Historic Connecticut (1944). Grosset and Dunlap, New York. (Text by Marguerite Allis.) Original copyright 1934.

Springtime in Virginia (1947). (Introduction by Virginius Dabney.) Hastings House.

Boston Landmarks (1947). Hastings House. (Text by Mark A. DeWolfe Howe.)

Behold Williamsburg (1947). Hastings House.

Mount Vernon, Virginia—An Illustrated Handbook (1947). The Mount Vernon Ladies Association of the Union. (Photographs only.)

Rockefeller Center, A Photographic Narrative (1947). (Hastings House.)

Invitation to Boston (1947). M. Barrows & Co., New York. (Text by Agnes Lyons.)

Churches of Old New England (1947). The Macmillan Company, New York. (Text by George Francis Marlowe.)

Fair Harvard (1948). Harvard University Press and Hastings House. (Introduction and captions by Donald Moffat.)

Open House in New England (1948). Hastings House. (Revised edition.)

Six New England Villages (1948). Hastings House.

Forty Acres (1949). Hastings House. (Text by Dr. James Lincoln Huntington.)

Salem Interiors (1950). Hastings House.

Princeton in Spring (1950). Princeton University Press and Hastings House.

North of Manhattan (1950). Hastings House. (Text by Harry Hansen.)

The Yale Scene (1950). Yale University Press. (Introduction and captions by Professor Robert D. French.)

Old Sturbridge Village (1951). Hastings House.

Beauport (1951). Hastings House. (Text and captions by Paul Hollister.)

Frontier of Freedom (1952). Hastings House. (With Henry N. Flynt.)

Who Lived Here? (1952). Little, Brown Co., Boston. (Text by Mark A. DeWolfe Howe.)

Bouquet de France (1952). Gourmet Distributing Corporation.

Cape Ann Through the Seasons (1953). Hastings House.

Cape Cod (1953). Hastings House.

Soft Skies of France (1953). Hastings House.

A Tour of Old Sturbridge Village (1955). Hastings House.

Nantucket (new volume under title) (1955). Hastings House.

The Berkshires (1956). Hastings House.

Southern Interiors of Charleston, South Carolina (1956). Hastings House. (With Narcissa G. Chamberlain.)

Mont Saint-Michel and Chartres (1957). Limited Editions Club printing of Henry Adams' text. (Photographic illustrations only.)

Italian Bouquet (1958). Gourmet Distributing Corporation.

Mystic Seaport (1959). Hastings House.

The Book of Boston (Volume I—1960). *The Colonial Period.* Hastings House. (Text by Marjorie Drake Ross.)

The Flavor of France (Volume I—1960). Hastings House. (Text by Narcissa G. Chamberlain and Narcisse Chamberlain.)

The Book of Boston (Volume II—1961). *The Federal Period.* Hastings House. (Text by Marjorie Drake Ross.)

The New England Image (1962). Hastings House.

British Bouquet (1963). Gourmet Distributing Corporation.

Old Rooms for New Living (1963). (Text by Narcissa G. Chamberlain.)

The Book of Boston (Volume III—1964). *The Victorian Period.* (Text by Marjorie Drake Ross.)

The Flavor of France (Volume II—1964). Hastings House. (Text by Narcissa G. Chamberlain and Narcisse Chamberlain.)

Historic Deerfield—Houses and Interiors (1965). Hastings House. (With Henry N. Flynt.)

The Flavor of Italy (1965). Hastings House. (Text by Narcissa G. Chamberlain and Narcisse Chamberlain.)

The New England Scene (1965). Hastings House.

Bouquet de France (new edition, 1966). Gourmet Distributing Corporation.

New England Legends and Folklore (1967). Hastings House. (Edited by Harry Hansen.) (Photographic illustrations only.)

Loch Tay, Scotland,
from *British Bouquet*

Chartres from the Wheatfields, from *Bouquet de France*

Hermival-les-Vaux

List of Illustrations

211

Farmhouse in the Poitou

The Roofs of Sidi-Bou-Saïd

Market Day in Dijon

Springtime in Venice

Chateau de la Morinière

Camogli

Courtyard in St. Raphael

General Index

Following this index is an index of names mentioned only. Places have been indexed selectively, and those mentioned in passing are not included.

Persons and Titles Mentioned Only

Places briefly mentioned are included whenever additional information
is found with the place name.

Académie Julien, 51
Achener, Maurice, 54
American Architect, 15
American Committee for Devasted France, 12-13
Ames, John, 15
Architectural Record, 15
Architecture, 15
Arms, Dorothy, 52
Arts and Decoration, 15
Atkeson, Ray, 120
Atlantic Monthly, 58, 84
Baroda, Maharani of, 64
Beach, Sylvia, 40
Beck Engraving Company, 162
Bone, Sir Muirhead, 44, 87, 119
Bonnard, Pierre, 198
Boot and Shoe Recorder, 9
Bourbon, Eulalia de, 54
Bradstreet, Anne, 138, 187
Brangwyn, Frank, 67, 119
Brasserie Lipp, Paris, 153
Brillat-Savarin, Jean Anthèlme, 155
British Museum, 44
Brock, H. I., 15
Bromfield, Mary, 64
Bunker, Dean, 86
Bunshaft, Gordon, 87
Caledonian Market, Boston, 136
Cameron, Sir D. Y., 44, 87, 119
The Century, 15
Cézanne, Paul, 198
Chambon, Albert, 153
Champsaur, Albert, 16
Charleston *News and Courier,* 166
Chez Garin, restaurant, 193
Chez les Anges, restaurant, 193
Chicago World's Fair, 51
Chorley, Kenneth, 138
Claire, Ina, 64
Clark, General Mark, 169
Colnaghi's, 44
Copeland, Charles Townsend, 84
Cotman, John Sell, 119
Country of the Pointed Firs, The, 138
Curtis Publications, 34
Czenkar, Eugen and Hermine, 106
Day, Clarence, 79
Dickinson, Emily, 138, 187
Dillon, Read, and Company, 13
Dodd, Francis, 119
Doelger, Mrs. Manolita, 175
Dunn, Harvey, 68
Dürer, Albrecht, 87
Eaker, General, 133

École des Beaux-Arts, 8, 10, 15, 18, 25, 26, 40, 41, 47, 67, 73
Edmunds, Frances, 164
Eisenhower, Dwight D., 126
Elizabeth, Queen of England, 134
Elworthy, Major Frank, 128
Emerson, Ralph Waldo, 8
Emerson, William, of Concord, 8
Farm Security Administration, 120
Ferber, Edna, 64
Filene's, 9
Fitzgerald, F. Scott, 40
Flandreau, Charles, 34
Florence, Italy, 171-172
Flynt, Mr. and Mrs. Henry N., 150
Foire Gastronomique, Dijon, 159
Forrestal, James V., 13
Foujita, 40
France, ship, 153
French, Robert D., 146
Galloway, Ewing, 120
Gellatly, Donald, 109
Gellatly, Mrs. William B.
Gellatly, Mr. and Mrs. William B., 30, 52, 79
Gellatly, Narcissa, 12-13, 15
George VI, King of England, 134
George's, restaurant, 172
Gielgud, Louis de and Mimi, 40
Gil, José Pedro, 54
Giuliani, Lieutenant Arthur, 122
Glaire, Abbé, 69
Gobo, Georges, 27
Goodman, Percival, 15
Grand Vefour, restaurant, 193
Griggs, F. L., 44, 71, 119
Guggenheim Museum, 40
Guiot, Marcel, 52
Haden, Seymour, 100, 119
Hamilton, Hamish, 162, 190
Harrison, Wallace K., 15
Harvard University Press, 144
Hassam, Childe, 144
Hemingway, Ernest, 40
Heritage Club, 118
Heritage Foundation, 150
Herter, Christian, 168
Hollister, Paul, 151
Hôtel Metropole, Taormina, 172
Hôtel de la Poste, Beaune, 107
Hôtel des Saint-Pères, 153
House Beautiful, 9
House and Garden, 15
Howard, Leslie, 64
Hutty, Alfred, 120
Huxley, Aldous, 40

Arques-la-Bataille

The Giant Oak

Etched in Sunlight has been designed by Samuel Chamberlain. The type used for text is Granjon, the display type Garamond, set at The Anthoensen Press, Portland, Maine. The photography, in fine line and 300-line-screen halftone from the original drawings, watercolors, prints and photographs, and the presswork, in off-set lithography, were done by The Meriden Gravure Company, Meriden, Connecticut. The paper is Mohawk Superfine Soft White Eggshell. Binding, by The J. F. Tapley Company, Moonachie, New Jersey, is in Holliston Roxite cloth, gold-stamped.